*The use of the word 'Nigger' in this book is solely confined to its historical context and usage, referring as it does to the name Guy Gibson gave his dog. It is not meant to offend or cause distress to any individual*

# Dambusters

*Simon Harrison*

J&KH Publishing

First Published in Great Britain in 2003 by
J&KH Publishing
PO Box 13, Hailsham,
East Sussex BN27 3XQ  England
www.aviationbooks.co.uk
enquiries@jkhpub.co.uk

1 3 5 7 9 10 8 6 4 2

Copyright   ©  Mediascope Ltd (2003)
Aston Science Park, Love Lane,
Birmingham B7 4BJ

ISBN     1 900511 61 4

British Library Cataloguing-in-Publication Data. A catalogue record for this book is available from the British Library.

Typeset in 10/13.5pt Latin

Printed in Great Britain by
Biddles Ltd

# Contents

# Foreword

The Royal Air Force Museum supports this new range of Dambusters product (DVD/Video/CD-ROM), including this book, to attract new generations of young people to share in our history and heritage. These products take an inclusive approach with the intention of making this important subject appealing to the widest audience possible.

*Dr Michael A Fopp MA FMA FRAes*
DIRECTOR GENERAL, ROYAL AIR FORCE MUSEUM

# *Preface*

This is the story of the bravery of nineteen young RAF crews, who risked their lives for an untried and untested low-level precision attack. Although the RAF had used low level precision attacks against German targets on previous occasions, including the raids on Augsburg and Le Creusot, it was the nature of this attack, conducted in darkness and using an unconventional weapon that made it unique in the history of modern warfare. 617 Squadron, better known by their nickname, 'The Dambusters', which the Squadron retains to this day, attacked their targets, the Ruhr and Weser Valley dams and rendered them useless for months afterwards.

The events of that night conducted by 617 Squadron, based at RAF Scampton in Lincolnshire, sent shock waves around the world. Churchill, in the United States for the Trident Conference, was received with exaltation in Washington when he addressed Congress on the 19th May. Newspapers carried reconnaissance photographs of the dam walls, showing in detail the accuracy of the Allied aircrews and the damage caused by the ensuing torrent as it cascaded through the narrow valley.

The popularity of the story of 'The Dambusters' is due, in part, to the 1954 film of the same name. Starring Michael Redgrave as the eccentric engineer, Sir Barnes Neville Wallis. Born of a humble background, the son of a doctor and one of four children in Derbyshire, Wallis was forever fighting the bureaucrats who, according to the screenwriters, blindly thwarted his every move to shorten the war with his magical 'bouncing bomb'. Richard Todd played the lead role, portraying twenty-four year old Wing Commander Guy Penrose Gibson. Born in India, Oxford educated and tragically killed at the age of twenty-six, Todd portrayed him as one of the lads and a supreme Pilot and leader. Together, Wallis and Gibson would destroy the German dams of the Ruhr Valley and seriously impair the industrial might of the German war machine, virtually stopping it in its tracks. Stirred by the exceptional theme tune and a magnificent story, the audiences were introduced to the legend.

All things considered, the film gives a reasonable account of the operation on the night of the 16th May 1943, bearing in mind that in 1954, the Official Secrets Act still prohibited the release of certain information concerning the raid. As a result, the filmmakers represented the 'bouncing bomb' as similar to a large football suspended beneath the Lancaster. This is a little strange when it was considered that the Germans knew about the weapon shortly after the attack took place, after securing a live, albeit damaged specimen, which despite reconstruction, was never used to its full capability. In reality, the weapon, code named 'Upkeep', was in fact cylindrical, resembling a roller or a large tin can. The portrayal of Gibson was also selective, for in reality, he was a tough leader with a fierce reputation as a taskmaster and disciplinarian. He was respected by the crewmembers of 617, but wasn't always the fun loving, outgoing individual that Todd portrayed in the film.

The dams' raid constituted one of the most audacious events of the war. The targets, the dams of Westphalia, provided the Royal Air Force with a challenge, one that it had not encountered before in any form of combat. The plan had officially been in circulation for three years, even before Wallis developed the idea and designed a weapon that would eventually destroy the huge structures. As early as 1937, it was believed that the destruction of the dams at the Möhne, Eder and Sorpe reservoirs would bring catastrophe to the heart of German industry.

The plan centred on removing the water supplied to both industry and the German domestic population. This would disrupt internal waterways and railways and bring to a halt the transportation of goods for the war effort to all parts of the Reich. It would also disrupt the area by inducing severe floods that would ruin industry and farmland. The idea was in place; but the Air Ministry lacked a method of making it reality. The breakthrough would come from a middle-aged engineer and scientist who worked for Vickers Armstrong – Barnes Wallis.

Wallis was in his fifties when he came upon the idea of the weapon that would deliver the devastating blow. Already responsible for the development of Britain's most successful airship, the R-100 and the hugely successful Wellington bomber, Wallis, after a series of mishaps and rejections, perfected the method of delivery and the size and shape of the bomb. Although the dedication that Wallis showed in the creation and testing of the bomb is unquestionable, he was helped enormously by Government officials, official Research Stations and Laboratories to perfect the bomb, which would on account of its operation, be more appropriately described as a 'reverse spinning depth charge'. Wallis preferred the term 'mine' to describe his creation.

The task of accurately delivering a mine during the attack would be the responsibility of the Officer commanding 617 Squadron. Wing Commander Guy Gibson was only twenty-four when he was given command of this operation, had already been awarded the Distinguished Flying Cross (DFC) on the 9th July 1940, (with a bar on the 16th September 1941). He was also awarded the Distinguished Service order (DSO) on the 20th November 1942, (with a bar added on the 2nd April 1943 after his final raids over Germany before joining 617). Already highly experienced, he acquired a team of crews from other RAF Squadrons to form the basis of the new Squadron and his responsibilities would include providing them with the necessary training to carry out their mission. The new Squadron, initially only known as 'Squadron X', before acquiring the official title of 617, was a combination of pilots from across the Allied forces. One American, several Canadians, Australian, New Zealand and British aircrew made up the force that would ultimately deliver this blow against Germany's industrial centre.

The intention of this book is to provide an in-depth account of 'The Dambusters', from their inception, through their training and the tests of the weapon, leading up the raid itself and the aftermath. The detail provided demonstrates the difficulty experienced in getting the project off the drawing board, the series of trials necessary to develop the mine and for the plan to be given the go-ahead. The training undertaken by the crews in order to prepare them for the mission, of which they knew nothing about until twenty-four hours prior to the attack, is also covered in great depth. This is complimented by the analysis of the events before, during and after, with reference to the Allies and from the viewpoint of the Germans. The conclusion demonstrates that the attack was not only justified, but also a huge success for the Allied Forces.

Several other books provide an in-depth understanding of the 'Dambusters' raid and are essential reading for a comprehensive understanding of the operation. Firstly, Guy Gibson wrote an excellent book about his experience of the raid, entitled 'Enemy Coast Ahead'. Unfortunately, published in 1946, it like the film could not reveal full details of the operation. Code names for the operation, alias names for those involved and other misnomers are all contained within the text, perhaps leading to some of those general oversights, which have occurred in the sixty years since the raid took place. However, it still remains an excellent and detailed companion to understanding the raid with a unique approach from a central character in the raid. The second recommendation is that book written by Paul Brickhill, simply entitled 'The Dam Busters'. This is an impressive literary piece, although written in the 1950's and so inadvertently containing misgivings and inaccuracies due to the stranglehold on official information. This publication also formed the basis of the screenplay for the 1954 epic movie. Finally, the excellently researched 'The Dam Busters Raid' by John Sweetman provides the most in-depth account of the raid available. The book is filled with technical data and provides an almost day-to-day account of the raid and is essential reading.

This publication is designed to offer an insight into the raid and to offer an accessible version of the story based on official uncensored material that removes many of the popularly believed myths and falsehoods, many of which are a result of wartime secrecy.

*This is the story of 'The Dambusters'.*

CHAPTER ONE

# 'Tripe of the Wildest Description'

The concept of attacking the heart of Germany's industrial powerbase was not new. Hugh Trenchard, the founder of the RAF and advocate of the bombing offensive against Germany in WWII, was quoted as early as the Great War as saying, "We must be prepared for long distance aerial operations against the enemy's sources of supply." The very idea of damaging, or better still, destroying the expansion of Nazi manufacturing, had been discussed years before the growth of Hitler's National Socialist Party State.

The roots, as suggested, can be traced back to WWI, with the increasingly long-range capability of bomber aircraft. The rise of the Third Reich naturally reinvigorated the discussion as to how the Allies could both conceivably damage German war production and the lower the morale of its citizens. The end result could also shorten a conflict and avoid the horrors that had been witnessed during the previous great conflict, some two decades earlier.

Vigorous discussions dominated the meeting rooms and corridors of the Air Ministry in 1938, during what proved to be the prelude to war in Europe. The discussions centred on identifying prominent targets for the RAF to be deployed against within occupied enemy territories, although much of its ferocity would be targeted specifically within the Third Reich's heartland.

The story of 'The Dambusters' begins in the secretive corridors and rooms of the Air Ministry between the period of the 15th to the 26th July 1938. This period witnessed identification of key areas in the German heartland, in particular, Westphalia and the industrial basin of the Ruhr Valley. The prime targets centred on the Mittelland Canal and the Weser Valley. The idea of attacking this area had been discussed and implemented into the 1937 Western Air Plans, a list of thirteen implementable plans to attack the enemy in the event of a re-ignition of war on mainland Europe. Perhaps the most significant was Western Air Five, a specific targeting of industry, including the supply of oil to the Rhineland, Ruhr and Saar industrial areas. Bomber Command, specifically, would target nineteen power plants and twenty-six coking plants, which it was considered, could bring the German industrial machine to a standstill. However, the desired effect could only be achieved with close to 3000 attacks and an estimated loss of 176 aircraft. The meeting of the Plans Operations' committee on the 15th July 1938 identified six dams situated at the heart of Westphalia, a province in western Germany. The major targets listed were the Möhne Dam, South East of the major city of Dortmund, the Eder Dam, South of Kassel and South East of the Möhne and the Sorpe Dam, South-West of the Möhne. In addition to these primary targets, three other dams, the Lister, Ennepe and the Diemel were all identified as important to German industry.

The proposed 3000 raids over the German industrial regions of the Ruhr, the Rhine and the Saar would have led to a massive loss of life, with virtually no sustainable damage to the intended targets. Other options had to be available, perhaps one which could incorporate newer aircraft and a weapon which could conceivably cause greater destruction, whilst utilising fewer bombers. A later committee proposed the attacking of two specific targets, the industrial and domestically important Sorpe and Möhne Dams. The potential damage and destruction that could be inflicted by successful raids against these centrally located targets would be much more detrimental to the Reich than 3000 raids, which were not guaranteed to deliver the successes warranted by such a huge mechanical and manpower undertaking. This is the first inclination of the Air Ministry's operational planning that eventually, would materialise as 'Operation Chastise'.

The Planning Staff realised that the dams would be a highly prized target and a coup for the Allied war effort, if they could be breached. The Germans would be aware of the importance of the dams for the continuance of their industrial war effort and so would have them heavily defended against attack from the outset of the conflict in 1939. However, reconnaissance photographs supplied by the RAF duly dispatched this rhetoric, showing that they were exposed and defended only by a few anti-aircraft positions and torpedo netting. It was thought that a number of expertly placed bombs could conceivably destroy these mammoth feats of engineering and bring chaos to the sunken valley areas below.

In July 1940, Air Marshal Sir Charles Portal, then Commander in Chief of Bomber Command, wrote to the Under-Secretary for Air, strongly emphasising the need to launch an attack against the German dams. Indeed, particular consideration should be given to the important Möhne: "The time has arrived when we should make arrangements for the destruction of the Möhne Dam. I am given to understand that almost all the industrial activity of the Ruhr depends upon the water contained in and supplied by this dam and if it were destroyed... great havoc would be wrought throughout the length of the water course".

Astonishingly, the British were not alone in considering the concept of dam destruction as an aid to curtailing a conflict. The Germans themselves were to reconnoitre British reservoirs as potential targets. It remains amazing that they seriously considered attacking similar British targets, whilst appearing to place little probability that the Allies would, or could produce a similar attack on their major reservoirs of the Ruhr Valley. The lack of consideration can be demonstrated by a communication sent by Justus Dillgardt, the Chairman of the Ruhrtalsperrenverin, the body responsible for the maintenance of the dams in the Ruhr Valley area, to the military authorities in the Munster region of Germany on August 29th 1939. In his correspondence, Dillgardt proclaimed his reservations regarding the state of the defences provided to protect the precious dams from being attacked by the enemy. He exclaimed that the dams could, potentially, be breached by the Allies dropping several high explosive charges into the water. If they were dropped with a level of accuracy, the subsequent explosions under the surface would produce devastating shock waves. This would weaken the structures, allowing huge volumes of water to surge through the subsequent gaps and cracks. In the valley below and with the force of the ensuing torrent, a man made tsunami would destroy, or at least severely damage, any object, house, bridge, railway or power station that happened to lie in its wake.

The area of the Ruhr Valley had a population of four to five million people, mainly in the villages, towns and cities that encircled the huge industrial area of Westphalia. Dillgardt's concerns went unheeded and even rebuffed on several occasions. The German authorities wrongly believed that their dams were untouchable, as the percentage rate of success from high level bombing against such a relatively small target was minimal. They believed an attack by low flying aircraft against such targets extremely unlikely, as they were supremely well hidden within the valleys and woodlands of the German countryside. All this contributed to the final decision that the anti-aircraft guns could and would be of more use protecting more vulnerable targets, such as ammunition factories and airfields. However, after further correspondence between Dillgardt and the military authorities in the region, it was decided to enhance the protection of the sites with a few more anti-aircraft guns and balloons. This was merely a gesture to appease Dillgardt and others in the Ruhrtalsperrenverin, as shortly after the last correspondence, they were promptly removed and relocated to more sensitive targets. This correspondence may well have been coincidence, but had the authorities taken Dillgardt's concerns more seriously, they would have unwittingly thwarted British attempts to destroy these primary targets.

The last two pieces of this elaborate jigsaw remained to be developed - the method and ultimately, the weapon itself. Many promoted their own ideas about how to destroy the targets. Suggestions ranged from the massive barrage of bombs and high explosives dropped from thousands of feet above the target, to an adaptation of a torpedo with cutters to allow it to scythe through the torpedo net obstacles. Both suggestions had their strengths and weaknesses, but were ultimately considered too inadequate or far-fetched to research any further.

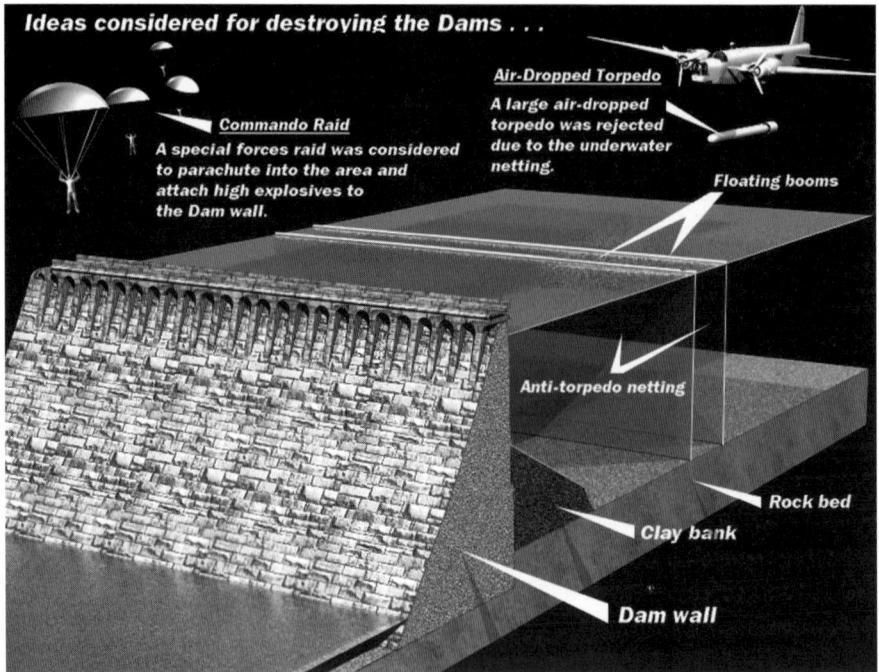

**Ideas considered for destroying the Dams . . .**

**Commando Raid**
A special forces raid was considered to parachute into the area and attach high explosives to the Dam wall.

**Air-Dropped Torpedo**
A large air-dropped torpedo was rejected due to the underwater netting.

Floating booms

Anti-torpedo netting

Rock bed

Clay bank

Dam wall

Dam showing torpedo-netting structures

Difficulties in designing a weapon that would deliver the results desired by Churchill and the Air Ministry would plague the experts right up until the operation was launched in May 1943. At the time, the RAF and Air Ministry favoured the use of small 500lb explosives in large quantities, in the belief that at least one of them would hit the target. Scientific thinking for the new weapon centred upon high explosive charges in the region of 10,000lb, twenty times the size of Britain's current largest weapon.

The Deputy Chief of the Air Staff, Arthur 'Bomber' Harris - well known for his dislike of hair-brained schemes and madcap inventors - replied to the comments made by Sir Charles Portal. The reply was, as expected, terse and straight to the point. "Attacks on dams...have been the subject of exhaustive study since July 1938. Thousands of pounds of explosive contained in one detonation would be required to destroy the dam. The only way to breach would be to drop a hundred or more M-mines together with a high explosive bomb. The practicality of which is insuperable at the moment".

The negativity of the correspondence, not even attempting to contemplate an attack on the dams, demonstrates again the thinking of Harris and his preference for a comprehensive bombing campaign. The use of specialist weapons on highly dangerous low level flying raids was impractical, according to the Air Ministry, because of the feasibility of success and the small numbers of aircraft available. The RAF had skilled and experienced flyers, but the

The brilliant Barnes Wallis (centre), designer of 'Upkeep' the bouncing bomb

challenge of such an operation weighted the odds heavily against them, particularly considering the equipment of the time.

Nevertheless, since 26th July 1938, the objectives had been clearly identified and the specific targets listed for consideration. The objectives were simple, destroy the dams in order to cut off, or at least disrupt, water supplies for both domestic and industrial usage. In addition, the attack would cause severe damage to railways, bridges and industry and prevent the navigation of the strategically important Mittelland Canal to Berlin.

The problem lay in ensuring that the target was breached. The precision bombing of any target was far from guaranteed, particularly against a target the size of a railway depot or ammunitions factory. The problem facing the

Allies was that the Möhne Dam was a mere twenty-five feet wide at the crest.

Barnes Wallis was in his early fifties when war broke out. A brilliant design engineer, he had worked for the Vickers Airship Company in London from 1913, before transferring to the Aircraft Division at Weybridge in 1930. Born in the Derbyshire town of Ripley, the son of a doctor, Wallis was one of four children, who, whilst a pupil at Christ's Hospital School, Horsham, excelled in Mathematics, English and the Sciences. After leaving education at sixteen, the young Wallis began working at the shipyards. Vickers recruited him, firstly as a marine engineer and later to his more familiar position in aeronautical design. Wallis had designed many notable pieces of engineering, including a British Airship, the R-100 and the famous Wellington bomber. By the outbreak of WWII, he was held the position of Assistant Chief Designer.

Wallis understood the flaws and shortcomings of the RAF's bombing arsenal and the attempts to build a weapon of more than 10,000lbs, which had not got beyond the testing stage. The newer, heavier weapons would require bigger aircraft to deliver them to the target. Wallis remembered the theory of shock waves and their destructive capabilities from an article he had read in 1935 concerning the problems associated with shock waves during the construction of Waterloo Bridge. The columns being driven into the Thames River bed were shattering because the pressure being inflicted onto the top of the piles sent shock waves into the bed, which in turn, would reverberate back up the column causing the pile to shatter. Wallis envisaged a bomb that could transfer this shock wave through a denser medium than air and effectively produce a seismic disturbance, like that of an earthquake.

He immediately set to work, learning about explosives and their effects from periodicals and journals contained in various libraries. Mathematical calculations brought Wallis to the conclusion that the current 10,000lb explosives used by the RAF would be insufficient. Immediately, he produced a sketch depicting a bomb, shaped in the style of his R-100 airship design. The new weapon would weigh in the region of 22,500lbs and be four feet in diameter.

Wallis met Dr W.H. Glanville, the Director at the Road Research Laboratory (RRL) in Harmondsworth, where he explained his hypothesis of targeting the Möhne and Eder Dams in Germany. Wallis explained that if heavy bombs were dropped by aircraft around the target, there was a reasonable chance that at least one would fall to within a distance of 150 feet from the dam wall. The explosion of such a large weapon would produce a shock wave powerful enough to cause a substantial breach in the structure. Glanville agreed to build mock scale models for the tests to be conducted. The first of many reports from the RRL to the Ministry of Air Production (MAP) was submitted in November 1940. The report outlined that the tests had been performed upon 1:50 scale models using exact dimensions. The report suggested that the testing stage had been progressing encouragingly. Tests had envisaged that severe damage would be inflicted upon the structure from a sole bomb, approximately 15,500lbs in weight exploding less than fifty feet from the surface of the wall. They continued with a scale model of the Möhne built in complete secrecy at Garston, near Watford. The tests were conducted outdoors and utilised three million blocks painstakingly attached together to form a miniature representation of the German dam. The use of explosives and distance in proportion to the scale model produced negative effects. The resulting explosions, measured between one and three feet from the face of the dam and two ounces in weight, damaged the model, but the structure held and the water remained in a pool behind the model.

Meanwhile, negotiations were underway with the Birmingham Water Company, who owned the Nant-y-Gro Dam, close to Rhayader in Powys, mid-Wales. The dam had been built to provide water for the construction of the larger Elan Valley Dams and was now redundant. The Ministry of Home Security wanted to secure the dam for testing purposes, which eventually could result in its destruction. On December the 27th, the Birmingham Water Company made the dam available and a proviso that the Nant-y-Gro would not have to be repaired should it be damaged was agreed. The Ministry of Home Security wrote to Dr Pye, Director of Scientific Research at the MAP informing him that the MAP must cover all the costs of experiments at the dam.

Wallis was sure, despite convincing evidence to the contrary, that a large, high explosive bomb dropped from an altitude of 40,000 feet would produce the desired effect and destroy its target. One problem still remained. At that moment, the RAF's ability to carry such a heavy payload was impossible. The aircraft available to them, the Halifax, Manchester and Stirling bombers did not have the capacity or lift capability for the weapon that Wallis envisaged. In response to this, Wallis put forward an idea for a massive aircraft capable of carrying the payload. The six-engined 'Victory Bomber' would, it was argued, carry more bombs and travel faster than a squadron of smaller bomber aircraft. The Air Ministry rejected this plan immediately. This was a purely operational decision as the Air Ministry pointed out to Wallis in a detailed letter. The letter confirmed that the idea of the Victory Bomber and a huge single bomb for it to carry was operational madness. The design of both were not yet off the drawing board and the development time meant that the expense of the new plane and bomb could conceivably be immaterial as the war could well be over by the time it became reality. In a meeting with Lord Beaverbrook, Wallis took the opportunity to put forward his idea for the super sized bomber aircraft that would be capable of inflicting massive damage on Germany. Beaverbrook listened intently to Wallis and asked for more detailed plans to be made available and Wallis immediately set about putting these plans on paper. The new aircraft would fly at extremely high altitude, making it invulnerable to German fighter aircraft. Its payload would consist of 20,000lbs bombloads and it would be able to fly in excess of 4,000 miles for any operation. Wallis provided Beaverbrook with the details that he required on the 20th July 1940.

Events were quickly gathering pace. Sir Charles Craven, Chairman of Vickers Armstrong arranged for Wallis to visit the Sheffield factory of the British Steel Corporation. Here, he was to discuss the plausibility of building a ten-ton bomb that would be able to withstand being dropped from a high altitude and explode. Wallis was now convinced that his theory would work and the dams of the Ruhr Valley would be destroyed and bring a swift conclusion to the war. A substantial report of the work was then completed, describing the work conducted over the previous twelve months. The treatise, 'A Note on a Method of Attacking the Axis powers' had eight substantial chapters, five appendices and two full-page diagrams. In this work, Wallis emphasised that the destruction of the dams would knock out the power and water supplies with devastating effect. Wallis introduced the theory that the destructive capabilities of a bomb were not in the initial explosion on the target, but rather in the power and damage it released from the shock wave.

Wallis then discussed targets and how an attack against hydroelectric power stations would cripple industrial production. In addition, the destruction of dams in key areas would create massive flooding in the region, including inundating a substantial number of important plants and infrastructures. In an attempt to ensure support for his thesis, he set about providing all interested parties both political and military, with the necessary information. It is unclear as to the truth behind a rumour that Wallis was visited by the Secret Service concerning mailing of his treatise to selected important figures. The story unfolds that the Secret Service were concerned due to a distinct possibility of a leak of top-secret information. However, according to reports, Wallis had distributed enough copies for a decision to be made that it was not exclusive enough to be considered a secret. The openness had ensured he indirectly protected the project's security.

The notes certainly produced the desired effect as far as Wallis was concerned, for almost immediately an official committee was established, which was led by Sir Henry Tizard, the scientific adviser to MAP. It was designed to advise the Director of Scientific Research and the Ministry of Air Production about the possibility of an aerial attack on dams (AAD). Essentially, this would develop into the AAD Advisory Committee and as a result, the experiments in Wales given the formal go-ahead.

The AAD committee did not meet until early March. The committee was reminded that plans for the attack on gravity dams had been under consideration for a number of years. Three methods were discussed in detail, consisting of an attack by torpedoes, attack by rocket bombs and finally, detonation of bombs in the water. Wallis' proposals met with some understandable misgivings and general scepticism and even at the very top of the 'chain of command', there were some doubters. Major Desmond Morton of the Prime Minister's Office concluded that the view from the experts was that the plan would not reach fruition until at least 1942.

Although Wallis was dejected, another plan emerged for attacking the dams. Professor R.V. Southwell suggested that a mine should be dropped into the water close to the target and detonated at a predetermined depth. Attached to a float, the current caused by the water approaching the sluice gates would ensure that it would attach itself to the target causing maximum damage to the dam wall.

Although Wallis' plans for a big bomb and the bomber to carry it were completely ruled out by MAP in May, there was one significant and influential supporter who indirectly persuaded and encouraged Wallis to carry on with his plans. Sir Henry Tizard wrote to Wallis regarding his claims and theory. There was little support for a single purpose ultra heavy bomber, but he did support the investigation of a ten-ton bomb. He also revealed that the official research concerning the effects of underground shock waves would be continued. The Victory Bomber plan was abandoned officially by Vickers Armstrong in September 1941, but Wallis was determined to prove himself right and the Ministry wrong concerning the destruction of dams.

After this set back, Wallis began to search for other means of destroying dams.

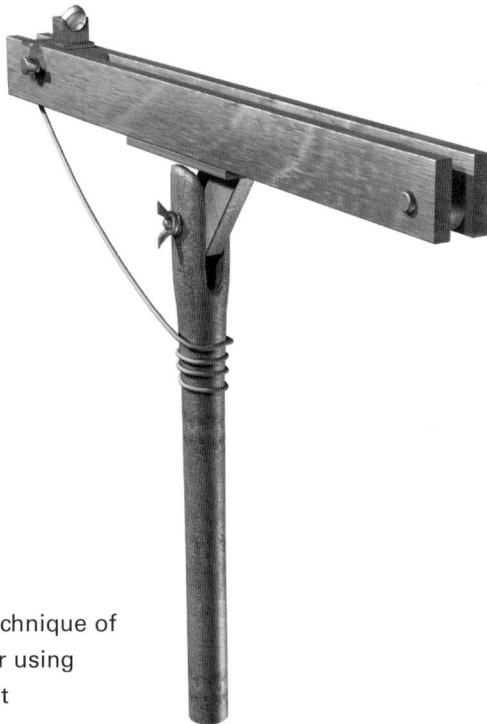

Wallis practised the technique of bouncing across water using marbles and a catapult

Aerial view of the Möhne Dam

He wondered whether a weapon dropped over the lake might ricochet and reach the dam in a series of hops. He remembered how in naval warfare, especially during the Napoleonic Wars, men would fire ammunition at enemy ships using shots fired from a cannon directly at the surface of the water. The angle that the cannonball struck the water determined the increased range of the projectile and Wallis' immediate thoughts were about testing this new theory.

At home in Effingham, Wallis, together with his young family, set about testing the hypothesis for a skidding projectile. The experiment centred on an iron bathtub, a catapult and a selection of the children's marble collection. His children were blissfully unaware that the extended recreation time with their father was the forerunner to future experiments which would eventually lead to the concept of the 'revolving depth charge', destined to destroy major targets in the following war years. Through experimentation, he began

Aerial view of the Eder Dam

The massive Eder Dam

to establish a law of ricochet and was able to control the height and distance of the marble's bounce. This theory was close to the plan put forward by Professor Southwell, but the accuracy of the weapon could be vastly improved and with the correct approach, the bomb would essentially bounce over the torpedo netting and carry on toward the target unhindered. When Wallis politely enquired as to the effect of a large spherical bomb on the surface of water, the reply he received was exactly what he wanted to hear - it would bounce like a football.

Wallis' idea could be the answer to the Air Ministry's dilemma. The relatively easy part of the experimentation was over and now Wallis had to work hard to gain official backing. Initially, Wallis approached the Admiralty with his idea as a concept for an anti-ship weapon. During the spring of 1942, further tests were conducted at the RRL at Harmondsworth to establish the size of charge required to destroy a dam wall.

By April 1942, Wallis was confident that his theory warranted the perusal of the Air Ministry. He claimed that a modified bomb bay on suitable aircraft would be capable of carrying a spherical payload. The weapon would be particularly appropriate for attacking dams, shipping and hydroelectric power stations. The bomb would, according to Wallis, creep towards the target and sink, with the detonation controlled by hydrostatic pistols, much like the depth charges used against German U-boats in the Atlantic. The 'bouncing' motion over a long distance could allow aircraft to deliver and depart the area long before standard defences came into range.

Both the Admiralty, who had long been searching for a weapon of this capability and the RAF were extremely impressed with Wallis' theory. Within a week, permission had been granted for Wallis to attend the testing tanks at Teddington. From the early results at Teddington and from the catapult tests at a lake near the Vickers works at Weybridge, Wallis decided that the most appropriate shape to use would be spherical.

Wallis only had a short time to experiment at Teddington. The site contained two huge water tanks, of which he used the larger of the two for the majority of his experiments. Due to the large amount of 'other' experiments being carried out, Wallis was restricted to around twenty days in total. It was during this time that the decision was reached to impart backspin into the testing process. Wallis had remembered how he painstakingly prepared and collated data regarding the effect of backspin imparted on golf balls. The chairman at Vickers Armstrong was an exceptionally good golfer and impromptu research by Wallis and others had determined from wind tunnel experiments, an estimate of lift force on a spinning sphere, which was essential to the ball bouncing on after it had initially hit the ground. Thus, by applying back-spin to the weapon would have some distinct advantages. Firstly, it would increase the distance of travel after release before hitting the water and secondly, stop the projectile plunging straight down after release. Finally, it would increase the range that the missile travelled after ricocheting off the surface.

The initial tests using spherical balls of various materials proved unsuccessful. Many cleared the tank completely and some others even caused structural damage to the building. In retrospect, Wallis thought it might be more productive to utilise a cylindrical shape. Tizard was the first visitor and was encouraged by the tests. The following tests were conducted under the scrutiny of Pye, Linnell and various members of MAP. One visitor was Rear Admiral Renouf, which was significant, because Renouf certainly had influence in the Admiralty and was immediately impressed with the results that he witnessed from the initial Wallis trials. Other distinguished Navy personnel arrived over subsequent trial days and for their benefit, Wallis deployed a model ship at the far side of the tank. When released, the projectile travelled toward the model before sinking directly underneath the water with the aid of the backspin. The Admiralty immediately researched the possibility of obtaining a version capable of being attached to the underside of a Mosquito bomber.

The summer of 1942 saw the first of the larger outdoor tests of Wallis' theory, which involved an anti-submarine mine detonated some distance from the wall of the Nant-y-Gro Dam. The first test was a failure, but an unscheduled test with a model at Harmondsworth had demonstrated that a charge detonated in direct contact with the wall would have the desired effect. As a result, a second test was arranged at the Nant-y-Gro Dam.

This test, watched by a large audience of specially invited dignitaries, was a complete success, with the mine exploding underneath the surface of the water in direct contact with the dam wall and creating a giant waterspout. Almost immediately, the effect of the resulting shock wave pushed the central point of the wall outwards, allowing the water to spill out through the resultant hole. Calculations suggested that a charge of 7,500lbs would be enough to create a breach and result in approximately seventy per cent of the water contained in the reservoir being released into the valley below. The weight of the weapon was also significant, for its capacity was well within the capabilities of an aircraft such as the newly introduced Lancaster bomber. The advantage of using a Lancaster would be significant due to the range the new plane could achieve. The calculations also provided an analysis of the scale of destruction that could be achieved using a mine in contact with the wall. It was now conclusive that a depth charge could be used to destroy the biggest dams in Europe. An answer to the long running question raised initially by the Air Ministry in 1937 had finally been proven in theory and was now within the RAF's capability.

The next stage was to conduct trials of a larger scale model of the weapon. These took place at Chesil Beach, near Weymouth during the period of December 1941 to February 1942. Initial trials proved disappointing, but perseverance proved that it was possible for the weapon to work successfully. Further trials were conducted and provided results that Wallis had hoped for.

Wallis had completed his second major treatise, entitled 'Air Attack on the Dams' by the close of 1942. Copies of this paper were sent to both the RAF and the Admiralty and explained in great detail his beliefs and the experimental results of the new weapon. The new report contained a significant section regarding the plausibility of attacking ships. The Admiralty and the MAP had now given direction to Wallis that the project for a smaller version of his weapon should be given priority. Wallis suggested that the preparation for trials involving a Mosquito aircraft would be ready within a few weeks. However, Wallis was concerned that the attack against the dams, the reason he had designed the weapon in the first instance, would be placed in severe jeopardy unless the proposed attacks against the dams and German capital ships were conducted simultaneously. The likelihood he feared, was that once the weapon's method of delivery had been revealed, counter-measures would be developed to ensure that it would be repelled the next time it was used, rendering it obsolete after a single operation.

Wallis used his new paper to conclude that the results of the Nant-y-Gro Dam experiments proved beyond doubt that it would be possible to breach the major German dams and destroy the industrial capability of the region. The Welsh dam was drastically smaller than the great Möhne and Eder Dams, but the experiments showed that it was the size and depth at which the charge exploded and not the thickness of the dam walls which would determine if they would collapse. It also seemed appropriate to clarify that current RAF aircraft would easily convey the maximum weight of the weapon.

The report showed that Wallis had developed a method of placing the depth charge against the structure, which against gravity type dams would be extremely destructive. However, a significant German dam, the Sorpe, was an earth dam with completely different characteristics. The concrete core was concealed within a massive, impenetrable earth bank at least 1,000 feet thick. This type of dam becomes self-destructing when a leak is made on the water-tight core, meaning that the Sorpe could possibly be breached if a charge was released upstream of the dam and at a significant depth. Once the concrete core had been breached, the earth structure surrounding the dam would be eroded away and the core itself would collapse due to a lack of support.

Wallis proceeded with a list of seven possible targets, all chosen for their importance to the region and the amount of damage that would occur if they were breached. The seven targets were subdivided into two distinct areas of the German industrial heartland. The first five possible targets identified were contained within the Ruhr Valley. These five targets, the Möhne, Sorpe, Lister, Ennepe and the Henne were all selected because they held a combined total of 254 million cubic metres of water. All of this was essentially for industrial and domestic purposes. Destroying these dams would, according to Wallis' theory, seriously disrupt the flow of major rivers, destroy or seriously damage the infrastructure and most importantly, deny vast areas of electrical power when the hydroelectric power stations situated along the banks of the river were destroyed by the torrent.

In addition to the targets identified in the Ruhr area, there were two important dams in the Weser area, the Eder and the Diemel. These two dams alone held in excess of 222 million cubic metres of water. The effect of destroying these dams, it was hoped, would seriously effect the levels of water that flowed into the strategically important Mittelland Canal. The consequence of disrupting traffic using the canal as a major route would seriously hinder the delivery of raw materials and completed armaments, like planes, trains and guns reaching their destination. The destruction of two power stations and numerous pumping stations would seriously diminish levels of production and deny industrial and drinking water to the numerous towns and cities in the area heavily reliant on the dams. Wallis commented that the destruction of the Möhne Dam alone would bring a serious shortage of water for drinking and industrial supplies and the destruction of the Eder would hamper the transport of goods in the Mittelland Canal.

Wallis continued with his paper, giving an explanation of his theory of a ship launched spherical torpedo or 'depth charge', which would be code named 'Baseball'. The longer range and speed of the projectile would provide the Navy with a powerful offensive weapon, which could be used against the German Capital Fleet in the North Atlantic. Wallis explained that the weapon would work in a similar fashion to 'Highball' and 'Upkeep'. The projectile, a circular steel ball surrounding a cocktail of high explosive, would be fired against the target. The backspin imparted would make the charge sink underneath the ship, cling to the hull and after sinking to its predetermined depth, explode with devastating results.

The conclusion of Wallis' paper reiterated that the dams of western Germany would be totally invulnerable to any current explosive charge deployed by the Allies unless it was deployed correctly against the dam wall and detonated at the optimum depth to induce a breach. Proudly, Wallis proclaimed that the proposition of a spinning bomb put forward by him would produce the desired effect.

During February 1943, Wallis spent precious time in meetings, conferences and dinners, with the major topic of conversation, unsurprisingly, concentrating upon the theory of 'Highball' and its effectiveness in Allied operations against the Germans.

A meeting of the Air Ministry, MAP and the Admiralty took place on the 13th February 1943. The committee of those present discussed the possibility of using the spherical bomb against targets, especially ships and dams.

Interestingly, Wallis was not present at this important conference. The meeting continued highlighting that two bombs were planned. The first, a small 950lb charge, which could be attached to the underneath of a small aircraft such as the Mosquito and be delivered against targets in shallow, calm waters. The other was a much larger 11,000lb bomb, containing 6,500lbs of high explosive for use against German dams and other targets such as locks. Lockspeiser indicated again, that in order to carry the new larger 'Upkeep' bomb, it would be necessary to modify the Lancaster and as such, it was the use of the smaller 'Highball' that was favoured by the Air Ministry and the MAP. It was agreed however, that all operations should be simultaneous to avoid jeopardising further operations in the future.

Air Vice Marshal Robert Saundby, Senior Air Staff Officer, Bomber Command, produced lengthy minutes regarding the meeting. In these he explained in detail the characteristics of 'Highball', which had been designed for the exclusive use against enemy Capital ships. Also, consideration was given to the development of a larger weapon, which would be used specifically against the German dams. A modified Lancaster could carry a bomb that if delivered correctly, would travel approximately 450 yards across the surface of the reservoir, before nestling against the side of the target. It would then submerge and detonate at the predetermined depth with the aid of hydrostatic pistols. According to the scaled down tests, destruction of the dam should be guaranteed if the weapon was detonated at around thirty feet and no further than ten feet from the target. The planned attacks, he continued, would require the allocation of one Squadron, effectively depriving Bomber Command of some of its strength for a number of weeks, in order to train the pilots for the special operation.

Wallis received the confirmation he needed during the following meeting of the Air Ministry on February 15th 1943. Wallis, supported by Mutt Summers, the Chief test Pilot at Vickers Armstrong, was informed that the committee had decided to allow the manufacture of one 'Upkeep' bomb and that in order to deliver the weapon during testing, one Lancaster would be modified and made available. The number of bombs and Lancasters would not be increased until the trials proved beyond doubt that the weapon could and would be a success. Wallis circulated a simplified version of his work, knowing that opposition remained towards the project, even though permission from the highest authorities had been granted for testing to take place. In the simplified version, Wallis emphasised again that 'Upkeep' was the only practical solution to the problem. A normal naval torpedo would lack both the penetration and explosive capability to achieve success. Wallis dismissed the idea that a charge could be floated downstream of the target due to the fact that such a delivery system was dependent upon the current, the charge staying in the middle course of the river and it not becoming entangled on the bank. There was also the possibility that the German authorities might see the explosive and safely remove it before it neared the intended target. There was only one option that, according to Wallis, would render all German defences futile and that was the 'bouncing bomb',

In light of the opposition against the 'bouncing bomb', a number of counter theories were drawn up. Lord Mountbatten was a keen advocate of the theory of floating a depth charge to the target. The celebrated Special Operations Executive (SOE) was already deployed in vast numbers behind enemy lines. They were responsible for uprisings, officiating over resistance and sabotaging as much of the enemy infrastructure as possible and were, it was thought, to be dropped into western Germany on an operation, code-named 'Cornet'. Whilst there, they would be instructed to place depth charges against the target and detonate them before retreating into the countryside. After much consideration, neither plan would be considered superior to the theory put forward by Wallis.

Air Marshal Arthur 'Bomber' Harris, Commander in Chief of Bomber Command was concerned. A letter sent to Saundby emphasised his concerns about the plans. The most worrying aspect seemed to be the requirement of a Squadron and thirty specially modified Lancaster bombers. The RAF could not afford to lose anywhere near that number on a foolhardy mission. It was, Harris complained, "perhaps the maddest weapon that had been proposed for some time" and his concerns continued with detailed reasoning as to why the mission would be a complete failure. The weight of the bomb was of major concern. It would be completely unstable when it began rotating and the merest notion of instability would destroy the aircraft and kill the crew. Harris was convinced, due to all the madcap ideas thought up by engineers and scientists he had encountered in the past, that there was a significant possibility that the theory would never become a reality. Problems would arise in ballistics, it would be impossible to retain any balance during the flight, targeting or on release of the weapon. There was also a chance that the weapon simply wouldn't work.

The success of the trials at Chesil Beach encouraged Wallis to approach Harris directly about gaining a commitment to the project.

Wallis journeyed to High Wycombe to meet Harris, armed with the mathematics and experimental results of his trials, as well as the cinematography that captured the trials at Chesil Beach. With the information under his arm, he stepped into Harris' office. Unsurprisingly, Harris was extremely hostile to the idea of the project, which he had so clearly rejected in the letter to Saundby. The sceptical Harris subjected Wallis to close cross-examination for some time. After this had ceased, Wallis, seemingly unperturbed, approached Harris with his calculations and detailed plan for attacking the dams. It was unclear whether Harris had yet made a distinction between 'Highball' and

Air Marshal Arthur "Bomber" Harris

'Upkeep'. This would seemingly explain his reluctance to release Lancasters against the target. Wallis, now on a roll, suggested that Harris view the trial films from Chesil Beach. He was impressed by the trial films and the information they portrayed. However, the doubts still remained. Harris' viewpoint would be changed by Chief of the Air Staff, Sir Charles Portal, who wrote to him explaining the Wallis theory in great detail. Portal finished his note by exclaiming that, "If you want to win the war, burst the dams." The notification was given that the trials should continue and that the modifications to two Mosquito aircraft were sanctioned. Three Lancasters were also sanctioned for 'Upkeep' trails, a further twenty-seven would be modified and 150 mines would be manufactured. Wallis was now faced with two major problems. The first was the design specification for the modified Lancaster had not been drawn up. This was a major problem, considering that it was essential that the bombs and Lancasters were ready for training purposes as soon as possible and be ready for the operation itself in May, when the reservoirs would be at their fullest. The second problem lay with the bombs. Wallis had not yet fully developed his design on paper and so no detailed drawings existed of the 'Upkeep' mine. Fortunately, both problems would be solved, with the drawings of the mine made available within the week, ready for construction and filling with explosive. Although details about the modifications had yet to be completely finalised, Avro began work on the airframes and bomb release mechanism, whilst Vickers would concentrate upon the arms which held the bomb, as well as the bomb itself.

It appeared that after years of application, Wallis' 'Upkeep' mine was finally going to become a reality. After many long hours spent in the tanks at Teddington, the trials with the Wellington and the late evenings preparing the information to present to officials, who may have influenced the decision to proceed with the project, it was finally underway.

CHAPTER TWO

# *Bomb Trials*

A meeting convened at Vickers House on the 25th August 1942, attended by the Air Ministry, MAP, the Admiralty and Vickers-Armstrong representatives, resulted in the decision to test a spherical bomb off the Dorset coast being given the green light. Prior to actual dropping trials a specially modified Wellington bomber, another of Wallis' technological triumphs, was flown to see the reaction of the aircraft when carrying the special load revolving at full speed.

December 4th 1942, witnessed what became known in official circles as simply the 'First Trial', at Chesil Beach, Weymouth. The Wellington, with the bomb bay doors removed and protruding arm structures on the underside of the fuselage carrying two weapons, took off from Weybridge. It was piloted by Vickers-Armstrong chief test pilot, Mutt Summers, with Bob Handasyde, also of Vickers Armstrong, positioned in the second pilot seat acting as observer. Wallis, acting as the Bomb-Aimer, crouched purposefully, nose pressed against the transparent Bomb Aimer's panel situated underneath the front turret, ready to release the weapon slung securely beneath the aircraft, at the correct moment.

Wallis scrutinised the water below in the fleet, searching for a suitably calm area where he could release the weapon and observe its progress. Allegedly the test very nearly ended abruptly whilst the crew were travelling to the designated test range. The story, although denied by Handasyde, revolves around the indistinct shape of the modified Wellington and its unusually shaped payload attached to the underside. It is said that a detachment of Naval gunners stationed at Portland on the South Coast of England, decided that the rapidly approaching aircraft could not be Allied, and so began targeting the mysterious object with the AA guns positioned at the site. Wallis, believing that the black plumes of smoke from the guns and explosions were resulting from a strange scientific phenomenon in the sky, perhaps caused by the weather, remained unperturbed until Summers banked the aircraft steeply to avoid having his wing ripped off. Safely away from the extreme range of the guns, the test continued with no further incident.

Wallis concentrated upon an area of water for the testing of the weapon. He directed Summers towards the zone and switched on the electric motor to begin rotating the spheres in the bomb bay. Both weapons were released, but the results were disappointing and the spheres disintegrated on impact with the water. The solution was to significantly re-enforce the remaining test weapons.

The next test, again planned for Chesil Beach, was earmarked for the 12th and 13th December 1942. Adverse weather conditions in the Channel prevented any testing until the 15th. The morning of the 'Second Trial' began as the first, although Summers, wary of the events off Portland eleven days previously, avoided the area fearing perhaps that they had been fortunate not to have been severely damaged, or even killed during their last encounter.

The planned test would involve the release of two trial weapons, one with a smooth steel outer casing; the other coated in a dimpled effect. The test was to see which would perform better under the conditions, undoubtedly having a massive influence on the final design of the 'Upkeep' mine that would go to the dams. Neither the smooth, nor the dimple-coated bombs had the desired effect, as they were badly damaged immediately after contact with the surface of the water. There was quite a gap to the next set of planned trials. The festive period was concluded and the trials resumed. The next trial was initiated on January 9th 1943, only five months before the attack would have to take place, when the reservoirs would be at their maximum capacity. The payload, a single revolving steel sphere modified and strengthened was released over the target range. Again, the weapon burst on impact with the water and a second test that day saw a malfunction in the weapon release mechanism, resulting in the weapon falling on land. The planned test for the following morning produced one enormous bounce, modifications were clearly needed. Vickers-Armstrong engineers prepared a wooden sphere for the next trials to be held on the 23rd and 24th January 1943. The official 'Fourth Trial' witnessed a miraculous and unexpected reversal of fortunes for Wallis. The weapon, rotating underneath the Wellington as before, was dropped from a height of forty-two feet above the surface of the water. The aircraft travelled at an air speed of 283 mph and the bomb had been given a backspin of 485 rpm. To the delight of Wallis and the others present, the bomb impacted with the water and produced a tremendous skip of several hundred yards, followed by repeated bounces across the surface. The weapon continued on its path reducing height and distance with every hop, until finally it disappeared under the surface. The resultant ripples left in the bomb's wake revealed that it has traversed thirteen times over its distance, which perhaps exceeded Wallis' calculations.

The next morning, a cameraman observed identical results. This time the weapon skipped across the surface approximately twenty times, clearing the defensive boom at the range. The results that Wallis had hoped for were not only witnessed by himself and Summers, but now there was indisputable evidence captured on film showing the potential of Wallis' idea.

On the 28th of January 1943, Wallis held a viewing of his trial film, entitled 'Most Secret Trial Number One' at Vickers House in London to an audience of high-ranking officials from Government departments, including Winterbotham, Barratt of the MAP and Air Commodore Faville. Later that afternoon he repeated the showing to others including Sir Charles Craven, Linnell, Summers, Handasyde and Lockspeiser. The following afternoon, the film was viewed at the Admiralty to an audience including the First Sea Lord, Sir Dudley Pound and his deputy, Admiral Boyd.

'Upkeep', with its wooden casing held together with metal straps, was to be quickly modified by Wallis

The response of the Admiralty to the new weapon was clear and the production of 250 "Highball" anti-shipping bombs to be carried by Mosquitoes was approved. However, what troubled Wallis was the lack of supposed interest from the RAF, especially as the concept for both 'Upkeep' and 'Highball' had originated from a desire to destroy the German dams in the Ruhr Valley. Unfortunately, the possibilities for this new weapon's use against naval targets appeared to have overshadowed the question of destroying the major German dams. It seemed Wallis met obstacles in every direction he turned.

The most difficult obstacle was convincing Sir Arthur Harris. Wallis, through Summers, who had known Harris for some years, arranged for a meeting at his Headquarters in High Wycombe, Buckinghamshire. Harris had earlier received some minutes from Saundby, to which he attached a copy of Wallis' 'Air Attack on Dams' paper. The reply from Harris was terse and to the point, leaving no doubt as to his thinking on the plan. However, it is likely that he had not entirely grasped the difference between 'Highball' and 'Upkeep'. "This is tripe of the wildest description…" he wrote. He argued that it would be much easier to attack the dam with a surface torpedo. "At all costs stop them putting aside Lancasters and reducing our bombing effort on a wild goose chase…This war will be over before it works and it never will."

Unknown to Wallis, support was beginning to build in favour of an attack on the Ruhr dams using the 'Upkeep' mine. Harris mistakenly revealed to Wallis that the green light had been given for three Lancasters to be modified to carry the 'Upkeep' mine for the new trials. A few days later, he had also been given the official go-ahead to utilise modified Mosquitoes for 'Highball' trials. These trials would begin immediately at Reculver Bay in Kent.

Apparently not everybody had been informed of the situation. Linell had instructed Vickers to inform Wallis that he was to cease any plans for the destruction of the dams. The Controller of Research and Development (CRD) had not attended any of the meetings held during the previous week and as such, had not been informed of the decision by Portal and Harris to allow the modification of three Lancasters, to be used in the trial. On the morning of the 23rd February 1943, Wallis was summoned to Vickers House in London for a meeting with Sir Charles Craven, Managing Director at Vickers-Armstrong. Wallis was told in no uncertain terms that work on the larger 'Upkeep' mine had to cease. The MAP had complained and the continuation of the plan would seriously harm Vickers-Armstrong's future interests. Wallis was therefore to "stop this silly nonsense about destroying the dams." Wallis, initially stunned, regained his composure and offered to resign. Craven jumped to his feet, repeatedly smashed his fist against the desk and cried "Mutiny". Wallis left the room. He met with Sir Thomas Merton, the Scientific Advisor to the MAP and former Professor of Spectroscopy at Oxford University and Sydney Barratt, who was Merton's assistant and had direct access to Churchill. That afternoon Wallis informed them that he had resigned and as a consequence the planned dams raid was cancelled. Merton and Barratt listened to and questioned Wallis for some time on the project. Group Captain C.E.H. Verity, in charge of AI3(C) the Air Ministry Intelligence Unit, received a mysterious phone call from his superior, Air Commodore Grant, Deputy Director of the Intelligence Office. The conversation revolved around a civilian engineer named Wallis, who would be visiting to discuss dates for a very special operation. He was to be given assistance and allowed to view highly secretive material.

Verity had been a Chartered Civil Engineer himself in the pre-war years. Wallis, armed with sketches and documents, arrived at his office. Verity was quickly enthralled by the idea, as the plan was not only absorbing but also quite brilliant in its execution. Verity's staff were highly qualified and so it did not take long for detailed plans and blueprints to appear, revealing minute details of the construction of the dams. The correspondence between Verity and Wallis soon gathered pace. Strangely, all letters were addressed to Wallis, care of the Effingham Golf Club, but contact was never made at either his home address or at Vickers.

Linnell called a meeting at his office on the 26th February. Present were Wallis, Verity and Craven. There they were told that the Chief of the Air Staff had authorised the testing of the weapon with a modified Lancaster to carry it. "The Air Staff have ordered that you are given everything you want."

Wallis had begun the first full size drafts of the 'Upkeep' mine by the 27th February. These were completed by the following afternoon for presentation to leading MAP officials and other important figures in the operation. It was decided that production of the steel cylinder and wooden spherical casing would be at the Vickers-Armstrong plant at Elswick in Newcastle-upon-Tyne. The Crayford plant would deal exclusively with 'Highball'. The completed cylinders would then be transported to the Royal Ordnance depots at Chorley, Lancashire for live mixture of RDX explosive, or to Woolwich in London for an inert mixture, which was a combination of cement and cork to simulate the weight of the high explosive, to be added. The first inert filled 'Upkeep' mine was then shipped to Farnborough in order for important balancing and ground testing on a Lancaster aircraft. The first 'live' flying trials using the modified Lancaster aircraft had now been arranged for early April 1943.

By early April the first of the newly modified Type 464 Lancasters were coming off the production line at Avro. The modifications saw significant changes to the Lancaster Mark III, the most significant of which centred on the removal of the bomb bay doors. In their place, Vickers attached the calliper arms and bearings that would carry the huge weapon 400 miles to its target. The second significant alteration on the Type 464 was the removal of the upper turret in favour of reducing the drag that the aircraft would undoubtedly suffer from having two protruding objects, one on the top and the other on the bottom of the aircraft. Too much drag and the aircraft would be handicapped by a lack of speed. This would be detrimental as it would make them more vulnerable to attacking fighter aircraft and it would reduce their operating range, as more fuel would be used overcoming the drag. Removal of the upper turret would reduce the aircraft's armament by a quarter. The first converted Lancaster arrived at Farnborough on the 8th April 1943. The second arrived at the Aeroplane and Armament Experimental Establishment at Boscombe Down and a third aircraft was eventually sent to RAF Manston. Soon, the first of the operational aircraft destined for 617 Squadron began to arrive at RAF Scampton in Lincolnshire. The delivery of the remaining twenty operational aircraft would continue steadily until 13th May 1943, just three days prior to the date of the operation.

The new trials were to be held at Reculver Bay, just beyond the Thames Estuary, near Margate in Kent. The area was secluded, away from civilian areas and surrounded by lush farmland. A well-known landmark, 'Reculver Towers', the remains of a twin towered Norman church dominated the site. Tuesday 13th April saw favourable weather and tide conditions in the area. The first test was carried out by Handasyde in the Wellington, who dropped the inert weapon at two target buoys. The impact made the wooden casing around the weapon disintegrate, but importantly the cylindrical mine carried on undamaged. The drop speed was calculated at 289 mph with a rotation of 520 rpm from eighty feet. Two more 'Upkeep' mines would be tested that day, the first, conveyed by Squadron Leader Longbottom in a Lancaster, was dropped from 250 feet. The mine disintegrated on impact with the water's surface. As dusk moved in across the Kent coast, Longbottom dropped the second weapon from fifty feet. The wooden support shattered once more, but similar to Handasyde's test of the morning, the steel cylinder continued to bounce across the surface for some considerable distance.

The 18th April saw Summers, the veteran of the Chesil Beach tests, drop three more 'Upkeep' bombs into the waters of Reculver Bay. Unfortunately for Wallis, he witnessed two sink without trace, whilst a third barely completed the trial. A decision was made to remove the wooden casing around the bomb. Wallis had witnessed enough in the early trials to see that the mine was completely effective without it, but bad weather prevented any further trials until the 21st April.

The modified 'Upkeep' mine simply had its casing removed

The next trial run was flown by the Avro Chief test Pilot Sam Brown, who had Handasyde alongside him acting as an observer. The first of Wallis' 'bare' weapons disintegrated and the test was a complete failure. Another drop the following day completed at a ground speed of 260 mph and at a height of 185 feet brought the same result. A tired and dishevelled Wallis pressed on determined to make his design a success. His extensive calculations led him to believe that the reasons for the previous trials' disappointing results lay in the fact that the speed and release height needed to be uniform. It would, Wallis believed, be more successful if the mine were dropped not from 150 feet, which the training aircrews could comfortably navigate, but a much more dangerous height of sixty feet. Flying at sixty feet in a fighter aircraft would be a massive achievement for an experienced pilot. To complete an operation at the same altitude in a large, four-engined bomber would be virtually impossible. The ground speed would also have to be altered to a frightening 232 mph. The crews had little time to become accustomed to their new orders.

The fourth 'Upkeep' trial was held on the 29th April. Longbottom was again at the controls as he carried the mine to its target and released the weapon as Wallis had instructed. From a height of fifty feet and a ground speed of nearly 260 mph, the 500-rpm of backspin induced by the four cylinder submarine motor and catapulted the weapon six times across the surface for a distance of 670 yards. The only drawback was that the weapon failed to maintain a straight course as it noticeably deviated by thirty feet. The same result was clearly visible on the following morning. Longbottom increased the height of attack slightly to sixty-five feet and reduced the speed of the aircraft to 218 mph. The 'Upkeep' mine covered a total distance of 435 yards in four consecutive bounces, its deviation was slightly greater at fifty feet to the left of its original course. Two days later, the weapon deviated forty feet off course. Again Longbotham had altered the height and attack speed and greatly increased the rotation of the weapon prior to release. The weapon travelled approximately 360 yards across the surface of the water with three distinct bounces.

On the 6th May, just ten days before the attack would take place, Longbottom flew four times with Handasyde as his observer. Wallis considered all but one of the tests a relative failure. As he supervised the realignment of the callipers on the weapon release system, he was concerned that this may well be the cause for the misdirection of the weapon towards the end of its test. Wallis did not have long before his theory was tested. Two separate mines were released on the 11th May. The first was dropped from a height of seventy-five feet at a speed of 230 mph. The second was released from a height of 500 feet at 245 mph. The former bounced five times covering a total distance of 430 yards with no deviation, the later cascaded for 450 yards bouncing six times. Again no deviation was recorded. It seemed Wallis' theory about the alignment of the callipers on the delivery system had been well founded.

The final test was conducted, for security reasons, off the coast at Broadstairs. The weapon was dropped from a height of seventy-five feet with the mine revolving at 500 rpm. The torpex filled bomb bounced seven times across the water's surface travelling a distance of 800 yards, before sinking beneath the surface to a depth of thirty feet and exploding.

The 'Upkeep' mine had now proven that it could satisfactorily absorb the impact with the water when dropped from a Lancaster travelling at 230 mph, sixty feet above the surface. It had also been proven, through a series of intense trials, that the mine could be released a distance away from its target to allow a sufficient period for the crews to evade the violent explosion that ensued when the hydrostatic pistols had been triggered at the predetermined depth. A final high-level release test on May 15th would prove that the weapon would not detonate from the shock of impact with the water. The weapon was ready.

'Upkeep' was a success for Wallis and the MAP, who could now implement their plans for destroying the German dams. The same could not be said of the Admiralty and their desire to add 'Highball' to their arsenal of weapons for use against the mighty German fleet, in the battle to bring food and supplies across the Atlantic. Reculver Bay also saw the independent trials of 'Highball'

Frontal view of 'Upkeep' installed under Gibson's Lancaster

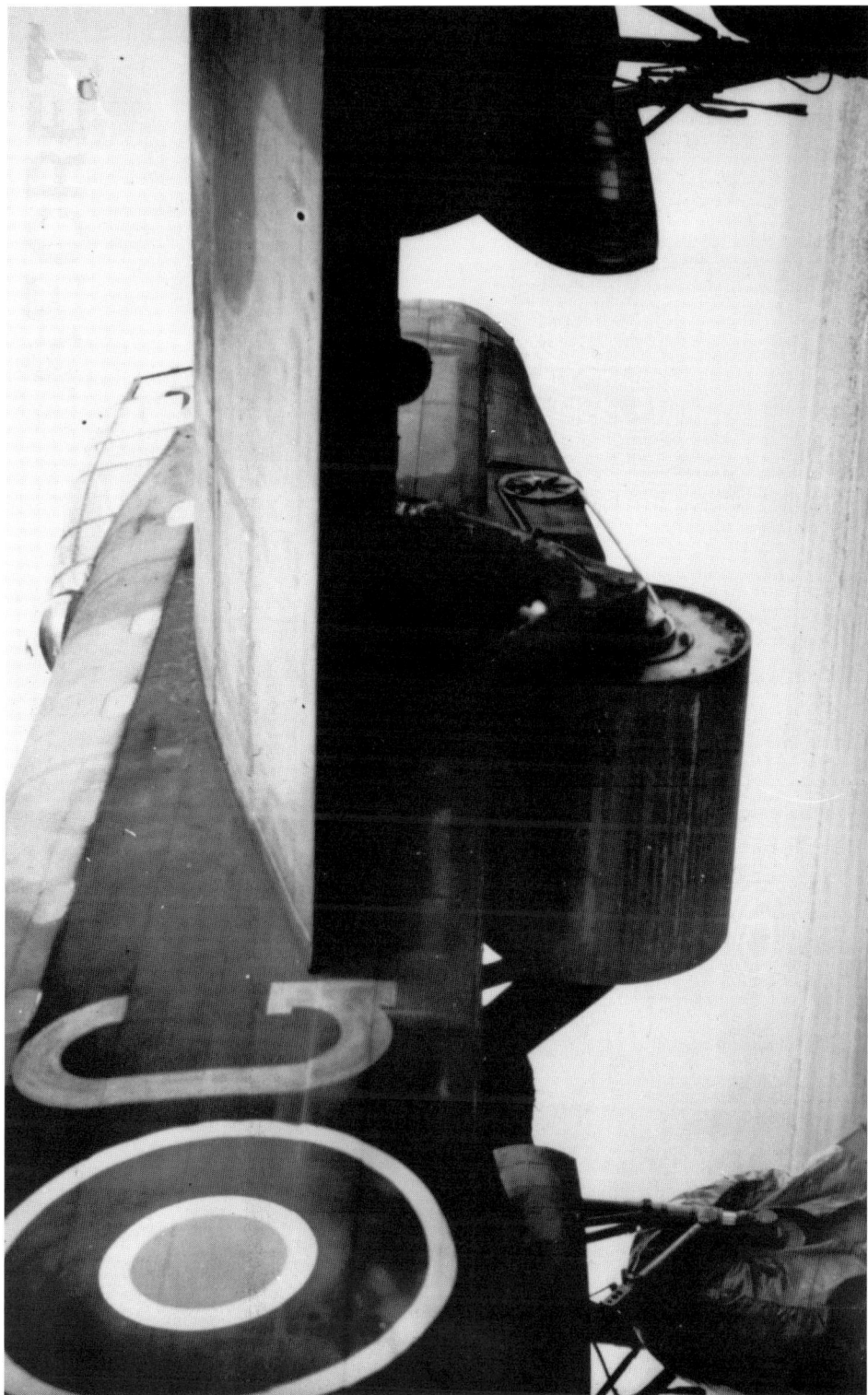

'Upkeep' held in place beneath Wing Commander Gibson's Lancaster

attached to the underside of the Mosquito bomber aircraft. The signs had been promising in the initial test stages. However, when further tests were carried out at Loch Striven in the Scottish Highlands on the 9th and 10th of May 1943, all three Mosquito aircraft experienced problems with the release mechanism and no successful tests were carried out. The fact that 'Highball' could not be perfected in time caused severe inter-service friction. The Air Ministry, desperate to use 'Upkeep' in the next few days when the conditions for the attack were optimum, argued that the shape and size of 'Upkeep' would in no way jeopardise 'Highball'. The Navy were not convinced and pressed for the project to remain under wraps until the testing of 'Highball' proved successful. It was decided that the stalemate would have to be adjudicated by the Chiefs of Staff who were at present attending a conference in Washington. Telegrams were sent arguing that the two weapons were unique and would not be compromised by being used on separate occasions. The weather and full moon conditions, as well as the fact that the water level of the reservoirs was now at its highest point of the year were central to the argument. The decision to approve the use of 'Upkeep' came after lunch on the 14th May, just forty-eight hours before the raid. The telegram stated the reasons that had been argued for the use of the 'Upkeep' separate to 'Highball' were sufficient for the project to go ahead.

CHAPTER THREE

# *Dambusting*

'U pkeep' and 'Highball' were weapons of unique design and composition. Never before had the RAF used such large bombs.

Wallis' larger mine was approximately 5 feet in length and 4.5 feet in diameter. 'Upkeep' had an unusual cylindrical size and shape, perhaps best described as resembling a roller from a steamroller, which gave it the ability to 'skip' across the surface of the lake toward its intended target. The bomb weighed approximately 9,250 lbs, of which two-thirds constituted the high explosive that would be used to breach the dam walls. It had to be, due to its proportions, carried externally lying across the aircraft rather than lying lengthwise inside the plane.

The term 'bouncing bomb' is a misnomer. The 'Upkeep' weapon was essentially a mine or an exceptionally large depth charge. The operation of the weapon depended not only on the accuracy of the pilots delivering it to its intended target, but also by the three hydrostatic pistols contained within the casing. The hydrostatic pistols had been the basic principle behind the depth charge and its success in defeating the German U-boats in the Atlantic.

The principal was simple - the 'Upkeep' mine's pistols would be set to a predetermined detonation depth of thirty feet. Experiments and trials demonstrated that the mine would travel in a series of tremendous leaps across the surface of the water, gradually decreasing as the weapon was slowed by the drag of the water. Upon hitting its target, the mine would effectively descend to its designated depth whilst the residual backspin kept it in contact with the face of the object, in this case, a dam wall. The hydrostatic pistols, already set to the detonation depth, detonated the main charge causing the shock waves that Wallis believed would destroy the dam.

Due to the secret nature of the weapon, the hydrostatic pistols were backed up by a fourth time delay self-destruct pistol. This initiated the moment that the mine was released from the aircraft. The failsafe was set to around ninety seconds, in order to guarantee that if the hydrostatic pistols did not detonate at the predetermined depth, then the weapon would self-destruct shortly afterward. The delivery of the weapon was in itself a massive operation,

# Anatomy of the 'Bouncing Bomb'

**Torpex explosive**
(6,600 lbs of underwater explosive compound)

**Endplates**
(One bolted onto each end of the outer casing)

**Hydro-static pistols**
(Fuses which detonate the explosive by means of water pressure)

**Cylindrical outer casing**
(Rolled drum made from 3/8 inch steel)

**Internal bracing**
(Six steel rods which help maintain the rigidity of the structure)

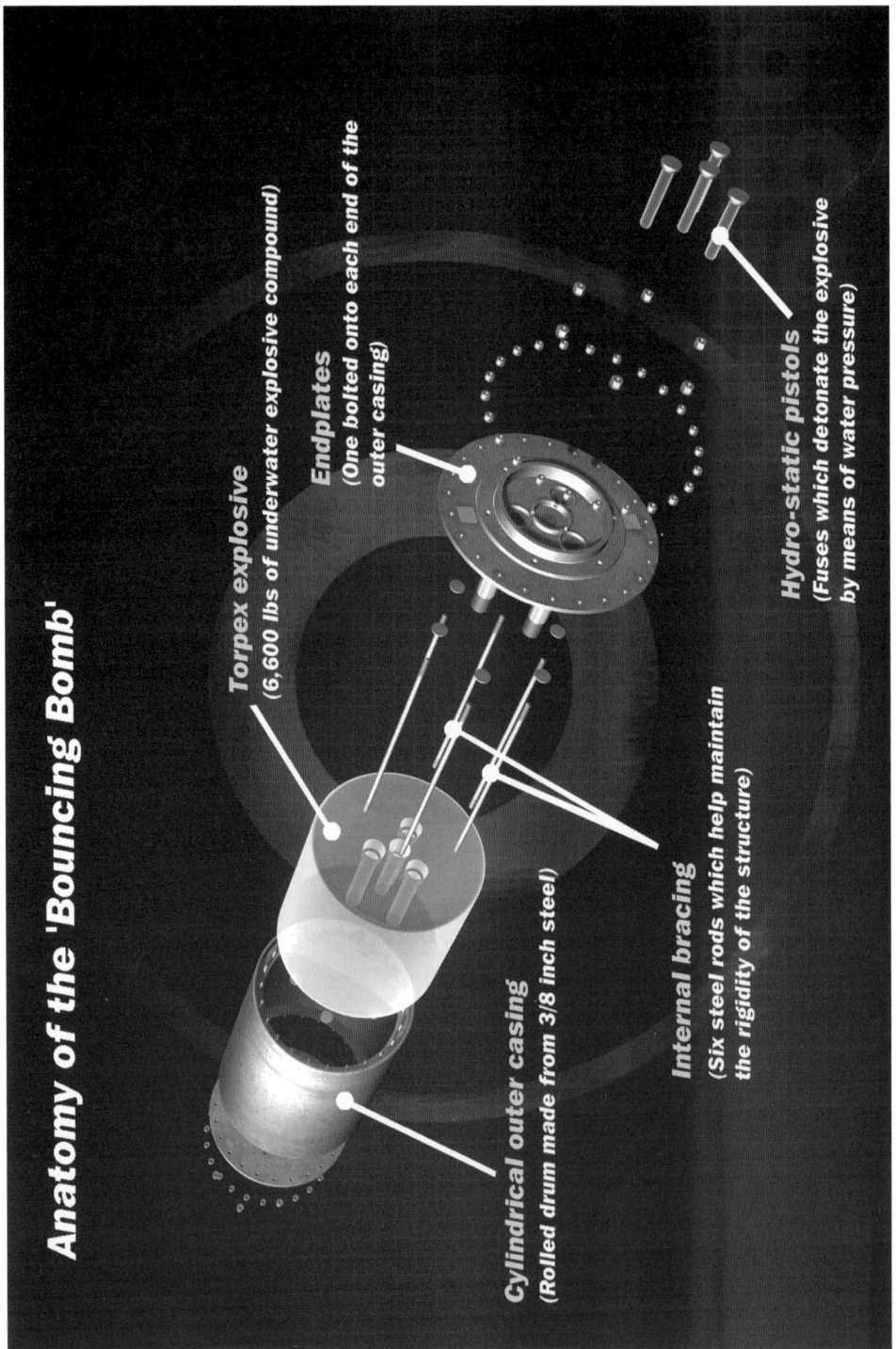

Schematic of the components of the 'Upkeep' mine

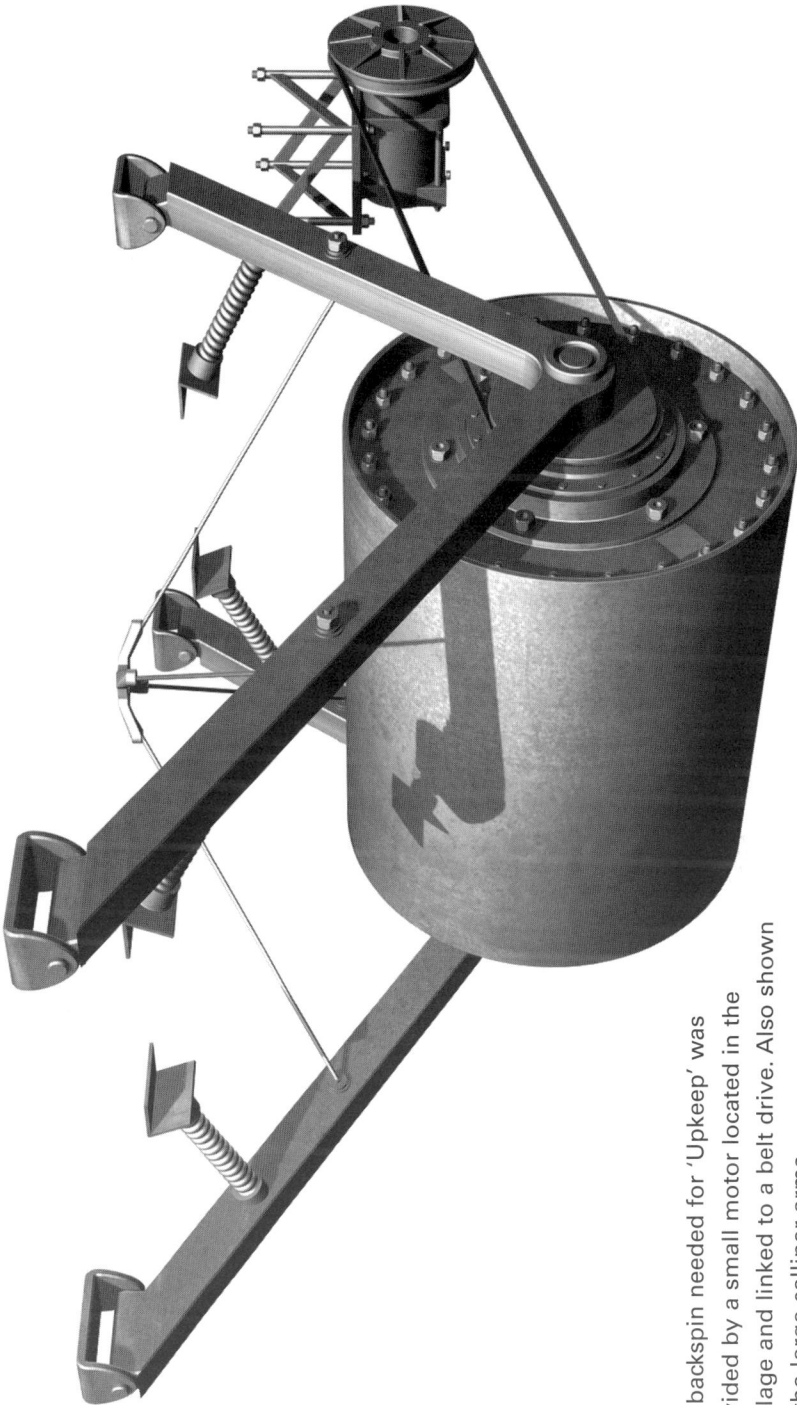

The backspin needed for 'Upkeep' was provided by a small motor located in the fuselage and linked to a belt drive. Also shown are the large calliper arms

both in carrying the weapon and accurately targeting the dam wall. Whilst the concept was being developed, the size and shape of Wallis' design was too heavy and cumbersome for use on any of the RAF's existing long range bomber aircraft. In 1942, the introduction of the newly designed Avro Lancaster, as previously discussed, provided the answer to the question of delivery. This aircraft with its large bomb bay and superlative load carrying capacity had not only the range to carry 'Upkeep' to the Ruhr, but also the performance and handling necessary for its release.

Due to the awkward shape and size of the new weapon, the Lancaster would require a number of modifications. The main alteration from the standard factory production Lancaster was the removal of the bomb doors. To hold the mine in the aircraft and allow it to spin freely, it had to be suspended by a pair of spring-loaded calliper arms, which opened to release the weapon.

The backspin, an important and integral part of Wallis' concept, was achieved by means of a motor attached to the fuselage. 'Upkeep' would be rotated at a speed of 500 rpm for a period ten minutes prior to release. The optimum height, speed and distance of the aircraft away from the target had already been calculated from the trials, resulting in an altitude of sixty feet with an approach speed of approximately 230 mph, some 450 yards away from the dam wall.

'Highball', 'Upkeep's' miniature relative was approximately half the size of its big brother. Unlike 'Upkeep', 'Highball' was designed for use by the high-speed bomber aircraft, the Mosquito. Both had a similar method of delivery. 'Highball' materialised from the original prototype of 'Upkeep' during the trials in late 1942. The Admiralty, extremely keen to remove the threat of the notorious German Battle fleet, in particular the battleship, Tirpitz, had been planning the demise of the ship, anchored in the relative safety of the Norwegian Fjords, where she posed an ever-present threat to the safety of the Arctic convoys. These convoys had been, amongst other duties, carrying supplies to the Eastern Front, in order to ensure that the Red Army could effectively engage the German divisions.

The Admiralty had seen the impressive first tests of the prototype weapon and Wallis had demonstrated that it was possible to target the weak underbelly of a battleship, where lack of armour protection made it vulnerable. Wallis' 'Highball', utilising the same technique as 'Upkeep', would traverse the surface and eventually slip beneath the water in close proximity to the target ship. The detonation, again set for a predetermined depth, would cause major damage to the underside of the vessel and the resulting hole would instantly flood with gallons of seawater. The importance of 'Upkeep' depended wholly on its ability to breach the huge German dams that the Air Ministry had designated as targets. Although the Ministry had identified five dams as targets for the raid, they regarded three as most significant. These dams, the Sorpe

## The Mohne and Eder Dams...

*A gravity type Dam is constructed as a tapering stone wall. Its solid stone masonry creates an immensely strong structure. The Mohne Dam for example is a 1/4 mile long and has a base width of 112 feet.*

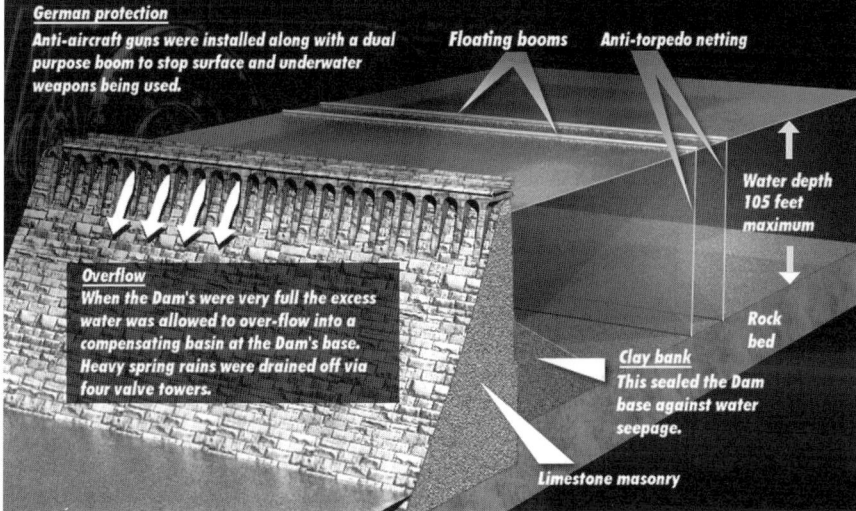

**German protection**
*Anti-aircraft guns were installed along with a dual purpose boom to stop surface and underwater weapons being used.*

**Floating booms**    **Anti-torpedo netting**

**Water depth 105 feet maximum**

**Overflow**
*When the Dam's were very full the excess water was allowed to over-flow into a compensating basin at the Dam's base. Heavy spring rains were drained off via four valve towers.*

**Rock bed**

**Clay bank**
*This sealed the Dam base against water seepage.*

**Limestone masonry**

Gravity type dam design, of which the Mohne and Eder are typical examples

## The Sorpe Dam...

*Earth type Dams have a much shallower profile than a gravity Dam. They are generally stronger because they have a much wider base, thus making them harder to destroy. The Sorpe Dam for example, has a base width of 1,010 feet, whereas the gravity Mohne Dam is only 112 feet. Earth Dams are often used in earthquake areas because they are not susceptible to shock waves.*

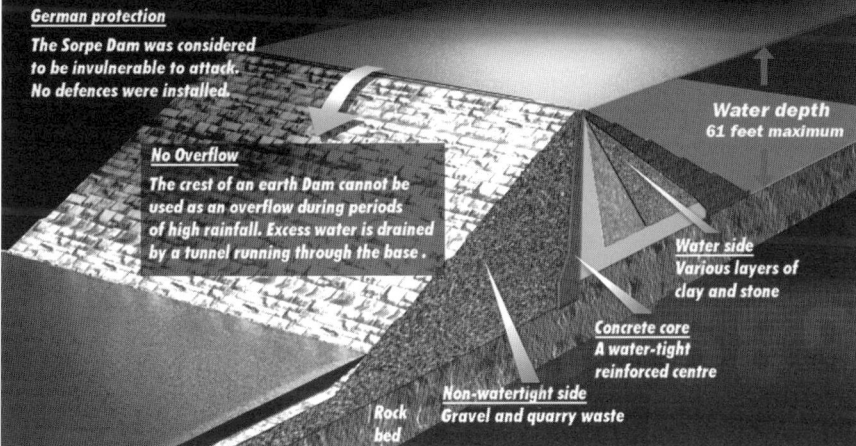

**German protection**
*The Sorpe Dam was considered to be invulnerable to attack. No defences were installed.*

**Water depth 61 feet maximum**

**No Overflow**
*The crest of an earth Dam cannot be used as an overflow during periods of high rainfall. Excess water is drained by a tunnel running through the base.*

**Water side**
*Various layers of clay and stone*

**Concrete core**
*A water-tight reinforced centre*

**Non-watertight side**
*Gravel and quarry waste*

**Rock bed**

Earth type dam design, of which the Sorpe is a typical example

(pronounced Zorpie), Möhne (Murner) and Eder (Ader), collectively account-
ed for approximately twenty-five percent of the Rhineland's water supply,
both to industry and domestic properties. The breaching of the dams would
see the destruction of houses, factories, railways, roads and bridges, bringing
communication to an immediate standstill.

The Möhne, a gravity dam, was situated twenty-five miles east of
Dortmund. The dam was responsible for holding back a huge reservoir, known
as the Möhne Talsperre, filled at times of high rainfall and providing the
towns of the Ruhr Valley with water during the summer months. The capacity of the reservoir was 130 million cubic metres spread across a surface area
just exceeding ten kilometres. As well as water supplies, it also powered the
hydroelectric plants situated along the River Ruhr. Two rivers fed the reservoir, the Möhne and the Heve. The water was carried through the dam as a
tributary for the River Ruhr, which it joined at the town of Neheim, approximately five miles downstream.

The construction of the dam started in 1909 and was completed within four
years. The structure, estimated to be 130 feet high from rock bottom and 112
feet thick at the base, decreasing to twenty-five feet at the crest, was constructed using local limestone rubble. This was specifically utilised to elimi-
nate the seepage that was often witnessed at dams of this type. The impressive structure was 2100 feet in length and the maximum depth of the water
was 105 feet. The dam's vulnerability to Allied attack by normal high altitude
bombing was considered minimal by the German authorities. The only protection afforded the site were a pair of torpedo nets situated in front of the
dam wall, with half a dozen light anti-aircraft guns placed at the base of the
dam and also on the twin towers that dominated the site.

The destruction of the dam would, according to official British documenta-
tion, create a shortage of domestic and industrial water, with the effects not
being immediately apparent for months. It would seriously undermine the
production of manufacturing materials, such as steel and coal, as well as disrupting power stations, hydroelectric stations, pumping stations and chlorinating plants along the length of the river. The destruction of the numerous
pumping stations situated along the entire length of the river would stop the
flow of important water reaching industries that relied heavily upon it to
manufacture materials. It had been calculated that in order to produce a single ton of steel, a plant would require between 100 and 150 tons of water.
Those factories, therefore, not completely destroyed by the onrush of water
would be deprived of essential water supplies. The disruption to industry
would see the production of aircraft, tanks and ammunition reduced dramatically for a period of time. Similarly, coalmines responsible for providing coke
to the region's massive furnaces would be flooded as the water entered the
deep shafts and coalfaces.

The inhabitants of the Ruhr Valley would also be affected. The destruction of essential chlorinating plants would create a desperate shortage of drinking water. The water contained in the dams would normally have to pass through numerous processes in order to remove the impurities and bacteria. The loss of essential drinking water would, it was hoped, weaken the morale and resolve of the German population.

The Eder, another gravity dam, situated at Hemfurth, six miles north of the village of Bad Wildungen, had a main purpose of providing water for the River Weser and the strategically important Mittelland Canal. It also stored winter rains and prevented flooding of the River Weser into highly populated areas. The reservoir did not supply water to industry or domestic properties. The capacity of the reservoir was a staggering 202 million cubic metres, making it by far the largest man-made lake in Germany. The structure was 139 feet high and 1310 feet in length. The thickness of the dam increased towards the base, starting at nineteen feet at the crest and reaching 115 feet at the base. The total surface area of the reservoir was twelve square kilometres with a maximum depth of 135 feet. The construction of the site was initiated in 1908 and took nearly six years to complete.

The destruction of the Eder would inundate with floodwater, the important industrial areas that had built up around the Mittelland Canal and the city of Kassel thirty-one miles downstream. The majority of the old city was situated on higher ground, but importantly, the tank and aircraft manufacturing plants were situated in the valley area and prone to flooding.

The final target considered as a high priority for destruction was the Sorpe Dam, located six miles from the town of Arnsberg and twenty-six miles from the town of Hamm. It held back a reservoir known as the Sorpe See with a capacity of 70 million cubic metres and was supplementary to the Möhne, thirteen miles away. The Sorpe was considered to be the most important dam in the Ruhr Valley for both industrial and domestic water supply. Its main purpose was to store considerable amounts of winter rainwater and supplement the Möhne in supplying the water to a high consumption area. Prior to its construction (and that of the Möhne), increased water consumption in the Ruhr area had led to severe shortages in the summer months.

The construction of the dam was different to the huge gravity dams of the Möhne and Eder. Construction started in 1927 and was completed in 1933. Comprised of a relatively small concrete core that was then surrounded by massive earth banks, 190 feet with a length of 1,965 and a thickness ranging from 33 to 1010 feet at the crest and base respectively. The surface area of the reservoir was approximately four kilometres with a maximum water depth of 200 feet. A roadway, 770 yards long ran across the crest of the dam.

The Ministry also considered this a significant target. Its destruction would not only cause substantial flooding in the Ruhr Valley area, in addition to the flooding from the Möhne, but would also deprive industry the water needed during the summer months. The Sorpe, like the other dams in the area, would take nearly two to three years to refill and would be emptied during the summer months, thus rendering it ineffective

The destruction of the three important dams, the Möhne, Sorpe and Eder, would seriously damage the production of essential raw materials for the war effort. The loss of industries producing vehicles and armaments would deprive Germany of the necessary military hardware it required to fight the Allies, especially the Soviets on the Eastern front. In addition, it was hoped that the loss of light, heat and water would diminish the resolve of the German people and of their belief in the Third Reich.

In addition to the three primary objectives, the Air Ministry had selected three other important dams to be targeted. The first of these was the Lister Dam, built between 1909 and 1911 and sometimes shown as the 'Attendorn Dam' in official publications. This masonry construction was over 850 feet long and 130 feet high. It had a curved face identical to the Möhne and contained 22 million cubic metres of water. It would be referred to as 'Target D' when the attack plans were drawn up before the raid.

'Target E', the Ennepe Dam was situated near the town of Hagen. The structure of the dam, built between 1902 and 1905, was similar to the Lister as it had a convex curve containing 13 million cubic metres of water. It was forty-five feet high and 1000 feet long with a road passing over the crest and was principally used to supply water for drinking and minor industrial manufacturing.

The sixth and final target was the Diemel or Helminghausen Dam. The structure was similar to the Eder and was situated on the River Weser, approximately thirty miles from Kassel. Providing drinking and industrial water, the dam was 131 feet high, over 600 feet long and held 20 million cubic metres of water.

The decision to attack these targets would be a tactical one made whilst the operation was in progress. They were classed as secondary targets, important in their own way, but less strategic than the Möhne, Eder and Sorpe. The decision to move onto these targets would only be made after the successful breach of the three primary targets and would also be dependent upon the number of aircraft yet to release their weapons.

CHAPTER FOUR

# *Chosen Few*

The steady stream of crews began to converge at RAF Scampton in late March of 1943. Although hand picked, not all the men who would form the Squadron were personally known to Gibson.

Wing Commander Guy Gibson (right) pictured with King George VI

Gibson (Middle, pipe in hand) with previous crewmembers of No. 106 Squadron, with Manchesters in background

Gibson and some of the crewmembers of 617 squadron. Back-row from left to right, Guy Gibson (6th), David Maltby (9th), Richard Trevor-Roper(13th)

Front-row from left to right, Mick Martin (3rd), David Shannon (4th)

Gibson arrived at the base on the 21st March. The selection method that he had employed is unclear, although many of the individuals and crews had flown together on numerous occasions previously, many more were not decorated, nor indeed had flown a desirable number of operations before recruitment to 617. Cochrane had little hesitation in selecting Gibson as his Commander for the impending operation. If one pilot could inspire his crews, it was Gibson. Already highly decorated and with a reputation for determination and ferocious discipline, Gibson had completed sixty-eight raids in bomber aircraft, the equivalent of almost three full operational tours. In between these bomber raids, the young pilot had been posted to night fighter duty protecting the skies over Southern England. This duty would see Gibson complete virtually one hundred sorties against German aircraft, intercepting the enemy before they reached their intended targets, bringing his total to nearly 170.

The crews arriving at Scampton were assigned on reputation and were by no means made up of purely British personnel. Twenty-one pilots were selected, of which nineteen would actually fly the Lancasters to the targets. Pilots included twelve from the RAF, five Canadians, one American, four Australians and a solitary New Zealander. This was a Squadron which would be influenced by men from all corners of the globe.

Gibson's crew consisted of a Yorkshireman named John Pulford, who would be Flight Engineer for the raid. Pulford had been recruited from 97 Squadron where he had completed ten operations. Gibson's Navigator was a Canadian Harlo Torgar Taerum who had successfully completed twenty-eight operations against Axis targets whilst stationed with 50 Squadron. The Radio Operator was a Liverpudlian, flight Lieutenant Robert Edward George Hutchison, recruited from 106 Squadron. He had been awarded the Distinguished Flying Cross (DFC) on the 12th February 1943 after completing thirty-three missions over occupied territory. The Bomb Aimer was an Australian Frederick 'Spam' Spafford who had been a fitter before the war. Originating in Adelaide Western Australia, Spafford, like Hutchison, had completed thirty-three missions against the Axis powers and had already been awarded the Distinguished Flying Medal (DFM) after completing fifteen missions in 1942 whilst serving in 50 Squadron. An Irishman, Flight Sergeant George Deering took the front Gunner position, who was serving in the Canadian Air Force, having emigrated some years before the war. Deering had plied his trade as a shoemaker before the onset of war, but after enlisting gained respect as an accomplished marksman. Deering had flown thirty-five bomber operations before joining 617. Flying Officer Richard Algernon Dacre Trevor-Roper completed the crew. Born on the Isle of Wight in 1915, Trevor-Roper served on numerous squadrons before joining 617, having flown over fifty operations and being awarded the DFM on the 23rd December 1942.

A Lancaster with its crewmembers

Three pilots came directly from 97 Squadron. They included one American and a New Zealander, Flight Lieutenant Joe McCarthy and Flight Lieutenant John 'Les' Munro respectively. Both pilots had earned their reputation as bomber pilots attacking targets over Berlin and Italy. McCarthy was twenty-three and from New York State in the USA. He joined the Royal Canadian Air Force (RCAF) in 1941, prior to his own country entering the war. He flew to Britain and was posted to 97 Squadron in September 1942. McCarthy would remain there until joining 617 six months later. The completion of twenty-nine operations whist serving in 97 Squadron would earn McCarthy the coveted DFC. Predictably, McCarthy chose to bring with him a large percentage of crew with whom he had managed to forge a relationship and understanding on previous missions in the preceding months. All but one of the crew had been with him on German bombing operations. McCarthy's Flight Engineer was a Canadian Sergeant named William Radcliffe. Radcliffe had joined the RAF in 1939 and worked as groundcrew before joining 56 Squadron in December 1939. McCarthy's Navigator was Flight Sergeant Donald McLean, a schoolteacher before the war from Toronto, Canada. McLean had enlisted in 1941 and had already completed nineteen operations before making the transition from 97 Squadron to 617 Squadron. The Bomb Aimer was Sergeant George Johnson who had completed one tour with 97 Squadron prior to his new posting. Sergeant Ronald Batson and a Canadian Flying Officer David Rodger occupied the two Gunnery positions. The only non-97 Squadron member was Leonard Eaton who would be the Wireless Operator on the mission. Eaton had arrived from 207 Squadron and had little experience compared to his new colleagues, each of whom had completed, or were about to complete at least one tour prior to relocation. Les Munro, a New Zealand farmer before the outbreak of the war, had completed a substantial number of operations over major German cities, including Berlin. Originating from Gisborne on North Island, Munro had joined the Royal New Zealand Air Force in 1941, before being posted to Britain and 97 Squadron in 1941. Munro would remain with 97 until the switch to 617 in 1943. Like McCarthy, Munro was able to call upon a crew of men who had flown together since December 1942. Only the Rear Gunner, a Canadian named Harvey Weeks, had not flown with in the same crew on any previous occasion. The Navigator, Francis Rumbles, Flight Engineer Frank Appleby, Wireless Operator Percy Pigeon, Bomber Henry Clay and Front Gunner William Howarth had joined 97 Squadron at similar times completing numerous operations together. The last of the three was David Maltby, an engineering student from Sussex, Maltby joined the RAF in 1940 soon after the outbreak of war and by the summer of 1942, the young pilot had distinguished himself on nearly thirty operations on various targets across occupied Europe. Maltby was awarded his DFC in July 1942. Again, Maltby had the luxury of bringing his own crew to the new

Gibson (on floor centre) with crewmembers and the brains behind the operation, Wallis (first row 2nd left) is seen next to Mutt Summers (front row 1st left), Roy Chadwick (Chief Designer at Avro) is second row from the front second from the right

Ready and waiting for action

Squadron. Every member, except for Victor Hill from Blackpool had served with 97 Squadron. However, it was only Maltby that had served with this unit for any period of time. In fact, he had been posted to 97 Squadron on two separate occasions. Astonishingly, all the other members had not joined Maltby until March 1943. In little more than a week later, they had been re-allocated to Scampton and 617.

Also present at Scampton in the early days of the Squadron were Flight Lieutenant William Astell and Pilot Officer Geoffrey Rice, who had been posted to 57 Squadron based at Scampton a few weeks earlier. Astell was born in Cheshire and had originally joined the Royal Air Force Volunteer Reserve (RAFVR) in the early days of the war, flying Wellington bombers from Malta against targets in the Mediterranean and later in the struggle in North Africa. Astell was awarded the DFC for his service before joining 57 Squadron. Along with Astell came his Rear Gunner Richard Bolitho from Barrow-in-Furness and his trusted Bomb-Aimer Donald Hopkinson, a reservist from Oldham, Lancashire. The remaining four crew included three from the Royal Canadian Air Force and a Scotsman. The important Flight Engineer position was held by a twenty-one year old Scot from Fife, John Kinnear, who had spent much of the war training. This raid would be his first major experience as a Flight Engineer. Three Canadians would hold the positions of front Gunner, Navigator and Wireless Operator, Francis Garbas, Floyd Wile and Abram Garshowitz respectively.

Present at the crew room with Astell was another pilot from 57 Squadron, Geoffrey Rice. Rice had completed his training and had been posted to Scampton. After a brief spell of three months with 57 Squadron, he was ordered to join the new Squadron. Rice brought four of his crew from 57 Squadron along with him. They included his Navigator Richard MacFarlane, who joined the RAFVR and Flight Engineer Edward C Smith from Berkshire. Rice also brought his two Gunners along with him. Thomas Maynard, a Londoner, who like MacFarlane, had joined the RAFVR, would assume the controls of the forward turret for the raid over the dams. The other, Stephen Burns from Dudley, which at that time was in Worcestershire, would be the Rear Gunner. These five crewmen were English and had flown on previous missions together. They had all joined 57 Squadron in December 1942. The two other crew members, Chester Gowrie and John Thrasher were Canadians.

These names were not the only crewmembers that would make the short switch across the airfield from 57 to 617 Squadrons. Squadron Leader Henry 'Melvyn' Young, was an exceptional pilot with two bomber tours to his credit. Acknowledged as an intellectual among his colleagues, Young would make the ideal second in command to Gibson. Born in the UK, Young spent a number of his formative years in Pasadena, California, before returning to the UK. The new Flight Commander had been educated in Britain and studied law at

Modified Lancaster with its top gun turret removed

Oxford and had rowed for the university in the first televised boat race on the 2nd April 1938. That year saw Oxford romp home in front of the BBC cameras in twenty minutes and by over two lengths from their Cambridge counterparts. Young had already completed service with other Squadrons, including both 102 and 104. The crew of Young's aircraft would be familiar to him. All but one, a Canadian Flying Officer Vincent MacCausland, the new Bomb Aimer had flown with Young whilst on 57 Squadron although they had only flown together as a crew for approximately ten days before transferring to 617. Navigator, Sergeant Charles Roberts, from Norfolk, Sergeant David Horsfall, the Flight Engineer, from Sussex, Sergeant Lawrence Nichols, the Wireless Operator, from Middlesex, Sergeant Gordon Yeo, from South Wales took the position in the front turret. Sergeant Wilfred Ibbotson, from Yorkshire completed the crew in the rear turret. They had all come together as a crew from 57 Squadron to fly with Young for the new squadron.

Flight Lieutenant Harold 'Mick' Martin from Australia would be the pilot of another crew. Awarded the DFC in November 1942, Martin had completed thirty-six operations by the time he joined 617 in March 1943. Martin's Flight Engineer was Pilot Officer Ivan Whittaker who had served under numerous other squadrons. The Navigator was another Australian, Flight Lieutenant Jack Leggo, who had been awarded the DFC on the 6th November 1942, after twenty-six operations. Taking the position of Wireless Operator was a young New Zealander, Flying Officer Leonard Chambers. A carpenter before the war, Chambers had completed thirty-one operations prior to joining 617. The first crew to come from 50 Squadron would be piloted by Squadron Leader Henry Maudslay, an old Etonian who had gained his DFC in January 1942 after completing a tour of duty with 44 Squadron. With Maudslay came his experienced Flight Engineer, Sergeant John Marriott from Derbyshire, who had chalked up twenty-seven operations flying with 50 Squadron before moving to Scampton. The Navigator was a Canadian Flying Officer Robert Urquhart, who had flown operations with Maudslay during the early months of 1943. The Radio Operator was Sergeant Alden Cottam from Alberta Canada. After joining the RCAF in March 1941, Cottam had flown numerous operations during his service, but only three operations with Maudslay over enemy territory. The Bomb Aimer was the recently promoted Pilot Officer Michael Fuller from Kent, who had served under both 106 and 50 Squadrons before selection to 617. Taking the position of Front Gunner was Flying Officer William Tytherleigh from Hove in Sussex and completing the crew was Sergeant Norman Burrows in the rear turret. A young trainee accountant from Australia, Pilot Officer Leslie Knight, piloted the second complete crew taken from 50 Squadron. After arriving in England in November 1941, Knight quickly established himself flying twenty-eight missions against enemy targets. Knight's Flight Engineer was Sergeant Raymond Grayston, an Englishman who had served with 50

Squadron since October 1942 before joining 617 in March 1943. Flying Officer Harold Hobday took the position of Navigator. From Croydon in Surrey, Hobday flew twenty-six operations with 50 Squadron and was promoted to Flying Officer on the 10th October 1942. The Wireless Operator was Sergeant Robert Kellow, an Australian from New South Wales who had arrived in England after training in June 1941. The Bomb Aimer was Flying Officer Edward Johnson, who was promoted to this rank shortly after assignment to 50 Squadron. He had a distinguished career before transferring with the others to the new 617 Squadron at Scampton. The two Gunner positions were filled by two Canadians, Sergeant Frederick Sutherland in the front position and Sergeant Harry O'Brien in the rear. Sutherland and O'Brien had flown with Knight on numerous occasions since the crew formed at the Operational Training Unit in 1942. Three other 50 Squadron crewmembers would participate in the raid flying in unfamiliar crews. The first of these would be Flying Officer Kenneth Earnshaw, the Navigator onboard Flight Lieutenant John Hopgood's aircraft. Alongside Earnshaw was his 50 Squadron colleague, Pilot Officer John Fraser. Fraser would take the position of Bomb Aimer in the crew. Hopgood's aircraft also contained two members from his old 106 Squadron, Flight Engineer Sergeant Charles Brennan and the Rear Gunner, Australian Pilot Officer Anthony Burcher. Alongside them were former members of the 44 and 49 Squadrons, Pilot Officer George Gregory and Sergeant John Minchin respectively.

The third member to switch from 50 Squadron was Sergeant Brian Jagger, the front Gunner in Flight Lieutenant David Shannon's aircraft. Shannon was an Australian who had gained his DFC whilst completing almost a tour and a half with 106 Squadron. This aircraft's crew was, like Hopgood's, made up of crews from different squadrons and as a result, had little experience together. Shannon knew Flying Officer Daniel Walker; a Canadian from 106 Squadron, but the remainder of the crew was brought in from elsewhere. There were two members from 57 Squadron already based at Scampton, a Scotsman, Sergeant Robert Henderson would be Hopgood's Flight Engineer and Flight Sergeant Leonard Sumpter from Northampton would be the aircraft's Bomb Aimer. The Rear Gunner, Pilot Officer Jack Buckley, completed the crew's compliment from Yorkshire, along with Flying Officer Brian Goodale, the Wireless Operator. They had arrived at Scampton after serving with 75 and 51 Squadrons respectively.

A large contingent of aircrew arrived in late March 1943 to Scampton from 49 Squadron. The 49 Squadron would in fact surrender almost two full crews to 617. The first of these would be the crew of Flight Sergeant William Townsend who had, at the outbreak of war, joined the Royal Artillery regiment of the Army before transferring to the Air Force. In little over a year, Townsend had become a proficient pilot and at the time of the call up to join

Majestic in its flight, the Lancaster was a very heavy plane to manoeuvre

617, had completed twenty-six operations and gained Flight Sergeant status. Joining Townsend was his Flight Engineer, Sergeant Dennis Powell from Kent. Alongside Powell was an Australian Navigator, Pilot Officer Cecil 'Lance' Howard who had come to England in October 1941 to complete training, before joining 49 in 1942 and completing one tour. The Bomb Aimer was another 49 Squadron veteran, Sergeant Charles Franklin from Hertfordshire. A car plant worker before the war, Franklin had also completed a tour before joining 617 in March 1943. Sergeant Douglas Webb and Sergeant Raymond Wilkinson held the positions of front and rear Gunners. Webb was born in Essex and had completed a tour of duty, whilst Wilkinson, a joiner before the war had complete twenty-one missions prior to joining 617. The only member of the crew who had not flown with the crew was George Chalmers. Chalmers had gained his experience whilst flying operations with 10, 7 and 35 Squadrons.

The 49 Squadron connection was continued by the arrival of Flight Sergeant Cyril Anderson. Anderson had flown nine operations since joining 49 in February 1943. Approximately one month later, he was called to join the new Squadron at Scampton. Along with Anderson came his Flight Engineer, Sergeant Robert Paterson from Edinburgh. Paterson joined 49 Squadron at the same point as Anderson and they had completed the nine operations together. The Navigator was an ex-teacher, Sergeant John Nugent, who had joined the RAF in 1940, joining 49 Squadron in late February 1943 along with the remainder of the crew. The Bomb Aimer Gilbert Green from Middlesex, Rear Gunner William Buck from London and William Bickle, the Wireless Operator, had gained valuable experience together as a unit, with the exception of the front Gunner, Sergeant Eric Ewan.

Other Squadrons that provided 617 with full crews were the 61 and 106 Squadrons. The latter would provide a Canadian Pilot Officer, Lewis Burpee. After joining the Royal Canadian Air Force in 1940, Burpee was transferred to England in September 1941 to complete his training. As a pilot with 106 Squadron, Burpee had completed twenty-six operations against enemy targets before transferring to 617 Squadron. Along with Burpee, the Flight Engineer was Sergeant Guy Pegler from Bath, who had joined 106 six months before in October 1942. The Navigator was an electrical engineer, Sergeant Thomas Jaye from County Durham, who had joined 106 in December. The Wireless Operator was a Pilot Officer Leonard Weller from Middlesex who had joined 106 Squadron later than the others. Weller was promoted to Pilot Officer shortly after joining 106 in February 1943. The final member from 106 was Sergeant William Long from Hampshire who had completed several operations with 106 after transferring in September 1942. The two other positions on the aircraft were the Bomb Aimer and Rear Gunner, which were both filled by Canadian officers. The Bomb Aimer was Sergeant James Arthur from

Ontario, who had enlisted in the Canadian Air Force in 1941 and the Rear Gunner was Flight Sergeant Joseph Brady from Alberta Canada. Brady had also enlisted to join the Royal Canadian Air Force in 1941.

An Australian, Flight Lieutenant Robert Barlow piloted the 61 Squadron contingent. Recently awarded his DFC after completing twenty-nine operations against German targets, Barlow was an accomplished and experienced bomber pilot. Alongside Barlow was his Flight Engineer, Sergeant Samuel Whillis from Newcastle-upon-Tyne. Whillis, like Barlow was an experienced flyer, joining 61 and ultimately 617 Squadron in 1943. The Navigator was Flying Officer Phillip Burgess. Only twenty years old when he took part in the raid, Burgess had only joined the RAF in 1941, but by November 1942 he had been promoted to the position of Flying Officer. Alongside Burgess was the Wireless Operator Flying Officer, Charles Williams of the Royal Australian Air Force. After completing his training in England, Williams was assigned to 61 Squadron, where he completed twenty-eight operations over occupied territory. The Bomb Aimer was a former solicitor's clerk from Cumbria, Sergeant Alan Gillespie, who had joined the RAF in 1940 and joined 61 Squadron in October 1942, where he completed thirty-three operations. The two Gunnery positions were taken by Canadian, Flying Officer Harvey Glinz and Sergeant Jack Liddell from Somerset, who had both completed thirty missions.

Sergeant Vernon Byers headed the contingent from 467 Squadron, a Canadian Pilot who had completed training and had been posted to 467 in February 1943. Byers' Flight Engineer was Sergeant Alistair Taylor from Scotland who had been posted to 467 at the same time as Byers in February. He had flown on just four operations prior to joining 617. The Navigator was Pilot Officer James Warner, who had joined the RAF in the early days of the war and completed operations over occupied territory, gaining a promotion to Pilot Officer in 1942. Sergeant John Wilkinson, the aircraft's Wireless Operator was from Cheshire. Since joining the RAF he had various postings before joining 467 on the 5th February 1943. Sergeant Arthur Whitaker had served with 467 since November 1942. He was an experienced Bomb Aimer with a number of key missions to his name. In the front turret was a Glaswegian, Sergeant Charles Jarvie, also with 467 since November 1942. In the rear, was a Canadian Sergeant James McDowell.

Further arrivals at Scampton included a crew from 207 Squadron. The aircraft would be flown by the experienced Pilot Officer Warner Ottley, who had completed thirty-one operations over occupied territory and as a result had been promoted to Pilot Officer in January 1943. Ottley's Flight Engineer was Sergeant Ronald Marsden from Redcar in Yorkshire, who had joined the RAF from school in 1935. Posted to 61 Squadron in October 1942, he had accumulated a number of operational hours before joining 617 in March 1943. The Navigator was Flying Officer Jack Barrett from Essex, who had been promoted to his present rank in July 1942. The Radio Operator was Sergeant Jack Guterman from Surrey who had flown over twenty-five missions with 207 Squadron since being posted there in November 1942. Flight Sergeant Thomas Johnston was the Bomb Aimer. Originating from Glasgow, Johnston had accumulated a number of operational hours prior to moving to Scampton. The Rear Gunner, Flight Sergeant Frank Tees had joined the RAF in 1941 and had served with various units before transferring to 207 Squadron in November 1942. In the front turret, was Sergeant Harry Strange from London, who had completed a number of sorties with 207 before moving with his flying colleagues to 617. The final group to fly on the dams' raid was piloted by Canadian Flight Sergeant Kenneth Brown. Born in Saskatchewan, Brown joined the RCAF in 1941, before coming to England to serve with 44 Squadron where he completed seven operations, being promoted to Pilot Officer on the 20th April 1943 whilst training with 617 Squadron. Brown's Flight Engineer was Sergeant Harry 'Basil' Feneron from Buckinghamshire. After several postings, Feneron was assigned to 44 Squadron in February 1943 before transferring again to 617 only one month later. The Navigator was Sergeant Dudley Heal from Hampshire. Heal would fly six operations against enemy targets whilst serving under 44 Squadron, having been posted to this unit in February 1943. Sergeant Harry Hewstone was the aircraft's Wireless Operator, who had worked as ground crew for 54 Squadron and had various postings before arriving at Scampton in March 1943. The Bomb Aimer was a Canadian, Sergeant Stefan Oancia from Saskatchewan. After enlisting in 1941, Oancia had various postings and taking part in six operations before moving to 617. In the front turret was Sergeant Daniel Allaston from Essex. Allatson arrived to 617 from 57 Squadron where he had been stationed since February 1943. An experienced Gunner, Allatson had also seen service with 279 Squadron and various other postings. In the rear turret was Canadian Flight Sergeant Grant MacDonald who had been posted to 617 from 44 Squadron.

These crews formed the nineteen which would ultimately take part in the dams' raid. Two other crews trained for the raid, but were unable to participate due to a combination of mechanical difficulties, a lack of airworthy Lancasters and some ill-timed illness. Flight Lieutenant Harold Wilson from Tottenham, North London, piloted one of the two crews that ultimately did not take part. Wilson arrived from 57 Squadron and had gained experience as a pilot in raids after joining the RAF in 1940. Wilson's Flight Engineer was Sergeant Thomas Johnson who had come from 44 Squadron, having served there since December 1942. An experienced Officer, Johnson had quickly gained promotion. The Navigator was Sergeant Clifford Knox who also came directly from 44 Squadron after completing several operations. The Wireless Operator was Sergeant Lloyd Mieyette from Canada. The Bomb Aimer was also a Canadian, Pilot Officer George Coles. In the front gun turret was Sergeant Trevor Payne from Gateshead. After joining the RAF in 1940, Payne served with 44 Squadron on two separate occasions in April and November 1942. He completed several operations before being posted to 617 in March. In the rear turret was Sergeant Eric Hornby who had seen action whilst serving with 44 Squadron since December 1942.

The second unfortunate crew who could not participate was that of Sergeant William Divall, a pilot from Surrey who had served with 57 Squadron at Scampton. Alongside Divall was Sergeant Ernest Blake from Bradford who had already served with Divall on 57 Squadron since February 1943. The Navigator was a Canadian, Flying Officer Douglas Warwick from Toronto. The Wireless Operator was Sergeant James Simpson. Having joined the RAF in 1939, Simpson had served with, 9, 613 and 57 Squadrons before selection for the 617 crew. Sergeant Robert McArthur was from Glasgow. The aircraft's Bomb Aimer, McArthur had several postings prior to joining up with the 617 Squadron quite late in April 1943. Sergeant Austin Williams took the position of Rear Gunner in Divall's crew. Originally from York, Williams was an experienced Gunner who had several postings prior to selection for 617 Squadron. These included both 207 and 97 Squadrons. Flying Officer James Rodger trained as a Navigator in Wilson's crew, but did not take part in the raid. Sergeant Buntaine was originally the front Gunner on Ken Brown's aircraft, but due to illness lost his position to Allatson.

# CHAPTER FIVE

# *Flying Lessons*

The first test drop of a full-size 'Upkeep' had yet to take place as the aircrew arrived at RAF Scampton in Lincolnshire. The weapon and its operation had not yet been finalised and the aircraft to carry it, the potent Lancaster bomber, was still undergoing special modifications to carry the weapon.

Air Chief Marshal Harris was reluctant to divert an existing squadron from the bomber offensive and Air Vice-Marshal Cochrane, the Air Officer Commanding No. 5 Bomber Group, had been given the task of setting up a new special squadron for the operation. His brief was to provide the crews, without reducing the effectiveness of other RAF squadrons. The dropping requirements of 'Upkeep', combined with the tactical elements of the operation required specialist skills. "Bomber" Harris had selected Wing Commander Guy Gibson to command this special unit. On March 17 1943,

Ready and waiting

Preparing for take off

fresh from completing his last tour of duty over Germany and looking forward to some rest and recuperation with his wife and faithful dog Nigger, Gibson was summoned to No. 5 Group Headquarters at Grantham for "special duties". Any thoughts that Gibson had regarding his holiday were instantly dashed as Cochrane outlined that a special operation was being planned and Gibson had been singled out to lead the attack. This was an offer that Gibson dare not refuse.

The crews, not all known personally by Gibson, were a mixture of already highly decorated and experienced flyers and those with less operational experience, but who had already demonstrated qualities of resolve and determination. They assembled at their new home curious as to why they had been removed from their normal squadrons and assigned to one so new, it had not even received its identification. In the meantime, it would be known as 'Squadron X'.

The Squadron was well established by the 31st March 1943. Crews had been arriving in small groups and individually since the 21st, but leave and other squadron commitments determined they would not all arrive en masse. Their first duties were to raid 57 Squadron for essential equipment and furniture and to begin the low flying exercises which would dominate their time at Scampton leading up to the raid.

On the 24th March, after a long journey by rail and road, Gibson was met at Weybridge station by Mutt Summers and taken to meet Wallis at his temporary office overlooking the golf course at Burhill. Embarrassingly, the new Squadron's own Wing Commander had not as yet received the necessary security clearance for a detailed synopsis to be provided by Wallis. The meeting allowed Wallis to describe the weapon to Gibson, but the young Wing Commander was not told the target for the weapon. He was, however, shown the trial films from Chesil Beach and he left the meeting contemplating likely targets for the new weapon.

Group Captain Satterly issued his orders to Gibson on 27th March. He would be required to lead his new Squadron in an attack against significant, but lightly defended targets. The attack would be planned to take place at low level, in moonlight, with a final approach to the target at one hundred feet and an air speed of 240 mph. Gibson was told that it would be convenient to practice for the attack over water. The afternoon of the 28th would almost see the end of the operation. Gibson, accompanied by Hopgood and Young, wanted to test the difficulty of flying at an exceptionally low altitude over water. The Derwent reservoir, near Sheffield, provided an ideal training area for low level simulation, due to its proximity to Scampton. Gibson conducted two tests, the first of which was completed successfully during daylight hours. The second, just after twilight, almost caused Gibson to commit himself and his two important crewmembers to a watery grave.

It would not be until the 29th that Gibson would receive confirmation of the targets 617 had been designated to destroy. Cochrane showed him two scale models, one of the Sorpe, the other of the Möhne. This allowed Wallis to expand on the information they had discussed previously. At least, Gibson mused, it was not an attack on the dreaded Tirpitz.

Gibson, on his return to Scampton, had already designated a list of ten separate routes for the crews to navigate, each being no less than three hours in duration. The crews roamed the fens of East Anglia and Lincolnshire at an altitude of between two hundred and five hundred feet. The routes were gradually increased to include other areas of the country. In his logbook, Flying Officer Robert Urquhart, Navigator aboard Maudslay's aircraft, noted that they had crossed the countryside at approximately five hundred feet, before reducing altitude to a mere one hundred feet, with an air speed of 240 mph, for a bombing simulation. The first week was intensive for the crews, with twenty-six cross-country flights undertaken at low altitudes and nearly 250 bombs dropped at the range at Wainfleet in Lincolnshire. All these flights had been carried out in daylight, but Gibson knew that the raid would have to be carried out in full moonlight conditions.

The major problem associated with this was a lack of moonlight conditions in which to practise. Other difficulties associated with night flying are the inability to accurately judge height and distance and the difficulty of accurately reading maps. Navigators were entrusted with guiding the aircraft safely to the target, regularly updating the Pilot with new coordinates to ensure that the payload could be dropped in the right area. The Navigators were used to plotting courses and direction finding from high altitude, where it was easier to locate known landmarks, such as lakes, canals and conurbations. The low-level operation about to be undertaken provided new problems. Fortunately, answers to these problems were provided during early April 1943.

The initial problem of night flying was solved by a training aid known as the 'Two Stage Amber Day-Night Flying System'. The windows of the aircraft were fitted with blue tinted screens and the Pilot, Navigator and Bomb Aimer wore blue tinted goggles. This enabled the crew to see their instruments in the cockpit, but the complementary colours created the effect of moonlight outside whilst flying in daylight. This allowed the crews to create a night-time simulation at any time. The system was first tested on 11th April and the first note of Gibson experiencing it comes from an entry in his logbook for 21st April. On 25th April, he and his crew used it for a long cross-country sortie at low level, culminating in an attack against Welsh dams. "The synthetic night flying equipment", as Gibson termed the invention, enabled the crews to complete a valuable few weeks intensive training. The only downside to the equipment was the length of time that it took the engineers to fit the filters to the windows in the aircraft. The windows in the cockpit were all unequal in

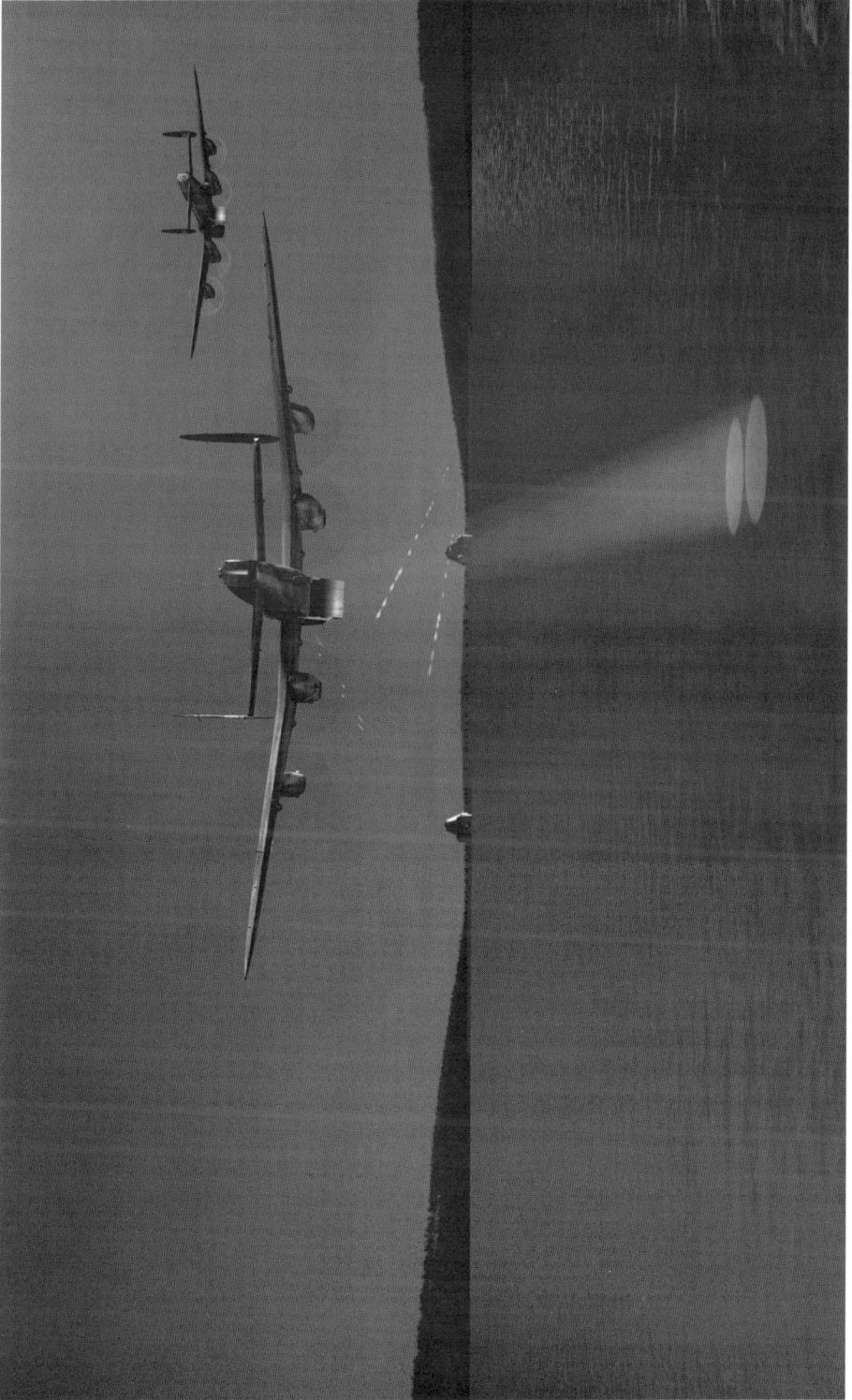

The light from the spotlamps (for height alignment) formed a figure of eight when at the correct altitude

Close up of the figure of eight

size and as a result, each filter had to be carefully measured to cover the glass correctly. The correctly sized panels were then attached to black linen hems in the machine shop and fixed securely into position. The process was made even more difficult because of the compactness of the cockpit area and having to work around the pilot seat and the instrument panels. Each conversion took several days and only six aircraft were so equipped.

The second important innovation solved the problem of accurately determining the aircraft's height over water. This was the brainchild of Ben Lockspeiser, the Director of Scientific Research at MAP, who adapted an idea with its origins in WWI. A lamp under the nose and one under the belly were configured to an angle that would converge to form a figure of eight on the ground or water, when the aircraft had reached its predetermined height. The Navigator would watch the spots of light from the cockpit blister and call out instructions to the Pilot. Squadron Leader Maudslay flew an aircraft to Farnborough, where a prototype installation was fitted and tested. Returning to Scampton, the system was tried by various crews over the airfield and their height checked from the ground with a theodolite. After a little practice, they could judge their height to within a few feet. The lights were originally set to converge at 150 feet, but when Wallis realised that it was necessary to reduce 'Upkeep's' impact with the water, they were adjusted to bring the height of release down to sixty feet.

By the end of April, the crews of the 617 Squadron had flown over 1000

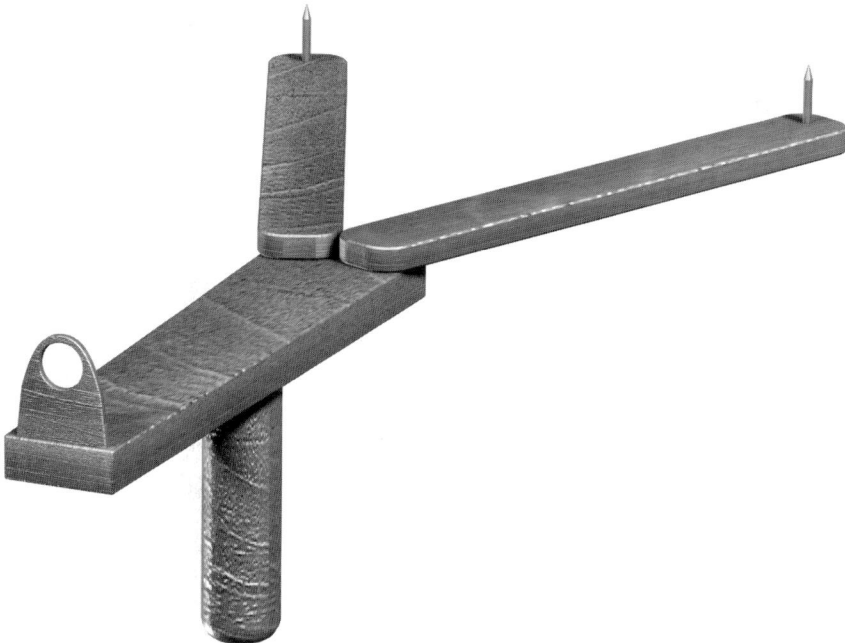

The very simple triangular shaped bomb alignment tool.

When a Lancaster had dropped its payload, the other members of the Squadron would support the attacking plane by drawing flak from the anti-aircraft guns

hours at low level. They were successfully overcoming the difficulties of low level flying and perfecting their long distance navigation at night, considered essential to locate and identify a relatively small target. However, the crews, especially the Bomb Aimers, had encountered another problem. They had found it difficult to determine the precise point of release for the bomb to hit the target. It was clear that a solution would be required to achieve the accuracy required by 'Upkeep'.

Wing Commander Leslie Dann was given the task of finding a solution. Again, the solution was simple and straightforward. Two nails would be attached to opposite corners of a triangular shaped piece of plywood.

The Bomb Aimer would place the third corner to his eye and view the towers of the target beyond the two nails. When the nails coincided with the towers on the dam, the weapon would be released. Crews began to practise and bombing accuracy improved significantly. Once the principle had been established, many crews found it easier to use a sight consisting of a length of string and chinagraph marks on the Bomb Aimer's blister, instead of the nails.

The training regime for April was intensive. Gibson's own logbook entries provide interesting reading. They show that he operated, like the other crews, on a rotation basis, due both to the intensity of training and the fact that the Squadron still hadn't received its full compliment of Lancaster bombers. On

The Lancasters flew so low, that occasionally the crews went underneath the cables of electricity pylons

4th April, he flew to the Derwent Reservoir (although he simply notes it as a lake near Sheffield) and the next day, he was piloting his crew on a low-level exercise over the Scottish Highlands. Four days later, he returned to Derwent reservoir and to Uppingham reservoir, correctly titled as 'Eyebrook reservoir', situated five miles south of Uppingham in Rutland. On the 11th April, he went down to Manston with Flight Lieutenant Bob Hay, the Squadron Bombing Leader, to observe the 'Upkeep' trials at Reculver. Whilst there, he took a single engined Miles Magister up for a local flight. Engine trouble caused him to force land the aircraft in a field. Gibson's log entry simply reads "Crashed in field. OK." He was airborne again on the 15th when he flew to Reading, Fairoaks and Weybridge to visit Wallis with Squadron Leader Longbottom.

The day of the operation was drawing ever closer. The crews were still unaware of the full enormity of the task that lay ahead of them, now just a matter of a few short weeks away.

The training at Eyebrook reservoir intensified. Up to ten aircraft at a time would converge on the target and swoop down to sixty feet above the surface of the water, which was an extremely low level for a large and heavy four engined aircraft. In addition, some of the most experienced crewmembers were suffering air sickness, due mainly to the added turbulence encountered at low level.

Day and night, the Lancasters flew low level across open countryside, their routes focusing on Eyebrook Reservoir or the Wainfleet bombing range. Initially,

Formation of Lancasters flying over rural England

residents around the Eyebrook reservoir reported that the Lancasters flew so low that many feared that they would collide with their houses. As the realisation dawned that they were in little danger, many people watched with increasing fascination. Similar events would also take place at Abberton Lake, listed in the official documents as 'Colchester Lake', approximately three miles south of Colchester in Essex, which was used in the later stages of their training.

Some crews did have near misses and occasional contact with treetops, resulting in aircraft returning to Scampton with evidence in the form of branches and foliage. There was a specific Intelligence Officer responsible for warning local authorities and military installations about low-level exercises in their area, but such was the intensity of training that the system did not always work.

Initially, the Squadron had been using ten standard aircraft borrowed from other squadrons, whilst waiting for the specially adapted Type 464 Lancasters to carry 'Upkeep'. These modified aircraft were slow in arriving from Avro and the first did not reach the Squadron until 8th April. Thereafter, they arrived at the rate of almost one new aircraft every two days, so that by the end of the month, the Squadron had fourteen. Of those that had arrived by 30th April, only nine had been completely modified. The others, under the supervision of Avro and MAP officials, would have to be completed on site at Scampton. The modifications to be completed included the fitting of the calliper arms and the installation of the spotlights.

Around the same period, the bombs began to arrive at Scampton. Fifty-eight 'live' weapons were delivered filled with RDX, a powerful new explosive and thirty-seven with an inert filling for training purposes. In addition, Scampton also received a ten-ton Coles' crane and six modified bomb trolleys, two mobile gantries and a selection of winches and lifting equipment. Before they could be used, each bomb would have to be mounted on a special rig and weight added to the end plates to ensure balanced rotation.

On 6th May, just ten days before the attack would take place, Gibson organised a meeting for all his pilots. He now had most of the designated aircraft at his disposal and so planned a night exercise for all the available crews in order to improve their navigation skills. Three groups of three aircraft would travel under his command to the Eyebrook and Abberton reservoirs via a specially planned route. There they would attack individually at sixty feet and a ground speed of 232 mph. Two other groups of three aircraft would operate under the same parameters, attacking the Derwent reservoir. The remaining crews, utilised like a mobile reserve, would practice their bombing over the Wash in Norfolk, using spotlights.

Gibson planned to control the attacks personally by radio. However, at low level the crews reported significant interference with the Lancasters standard wireless equipment. On 7th May, it was decided to fit each Lancaster with the

VHF units used on fighter aircraft. Seven representatives from Farnborough, one officer and thirty-five men from No. 26 Signals Group were sent to Scampton and despite the complexities of the task, successfully completed it inside three days. Air Vice-Marshal Cochrane reported that the sets had been fitted to all eighteen available aircraft by 1730 hours on 9th May. He commented that the operation "indicates the drive and enthusiasm with which this apparently impossible task was handled."

Meanwhile, No. 5 Group had drawn up detailed plans for the operation, which were passed to Gibson for comment. Gibson wanted to change the target designation from 'XYZ' to 'ABC', in accordance with the routine the crews had become accustomed to during the few weeks they had been together. Twenty aircraft were scheduled to carry out the attack. A first wave of nine aircraft would take off in three groups at ten minute intervals, followed by the remaining eleven aircraft at three minute intervals thereafter. Fifteen aircraft would attack targets A, B and C in order, only moving onto the next as each target was breached. At the same time five aircraft would attack Target C. Gibson agreed that the crews should cross the North Sea at sixty feet, but disagreed with the plan to authorise the pilots to climb a few thousand feet when nearing the Dutch coast in order to confirm their position. It was imperative, Gibson argued, that the crews remain low to avoid contact with enemy night fighters. The formation leader should climb to 500 feet to pinpoint landmarks for navigation, but should then immediately return to low level until close to the target, where he should then climb up to 1000 feet. After the completion of the task, all remaining aircraft should return to Scampton by "widely divergent" routes, remaining at low level until successfully across the North Sea.

Even as the operation was being meticulously planned, it was not clear if the 'Upkeep' mine would be ready for the operation. Gibson tested the weapon from his Lancaster on 11th May, noting that the mine was dropped from sixty feet and produced a run of 600 yards. Selected crews of 617 Squadron flew down to Reculver to experience the effect of 'Upkeep' on their aircraft and to release an inert weapon. Shannon, Munro and Knight went down on May 12th. Official observers witnessed the weapons drop from the correct height and approach speed, bounce across the surface for a good distance and then roll up the beach. Munro however, delivered his weapon from lower than sixty feet and felt his aircraft shudder, as the water thrown up from the weapon's initial impact with the water surface damaged his tail plane. Fortunately for Munro, the damage was not extensive and his aircraft was repairable. This wasn't the case with the Lancaster piloted by Squadron Leader Maudslay. His mishap caused greater damage to the aircraft and although he landed safely, it was impossible to repair the damage in time for the raid and he was allotted another aircraft. The Squadron was down to nineteen aircraft and twenty-one crews.

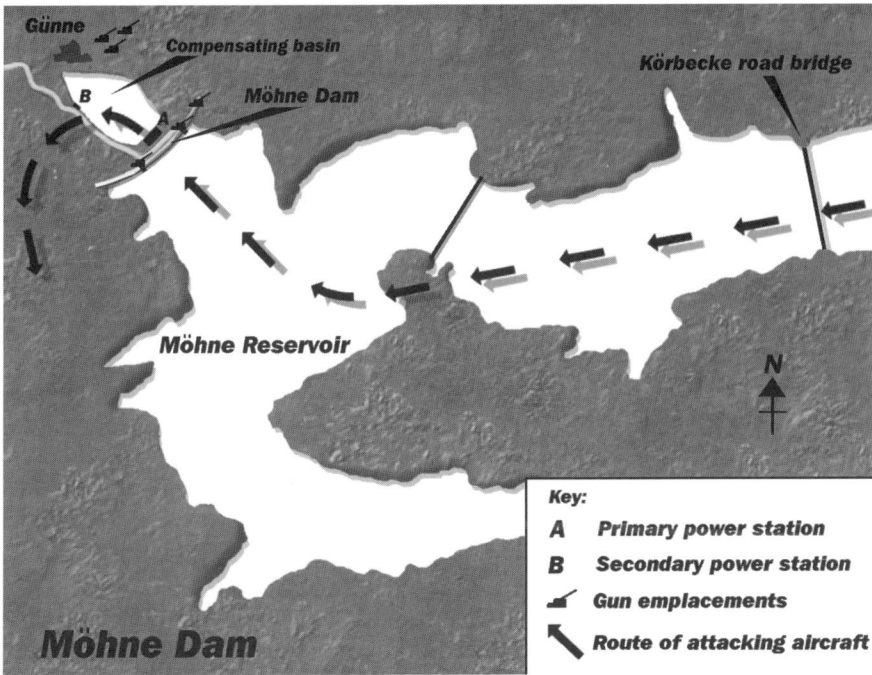

**Günne**
**Compensating basin**
**Körbecke road bridge**
**B**
**Möhne Dam**
**A**
**Möhne Reservoir**
**N**

**Key:**
**A**    **Primary power station**
**B**    **Secondary power station**
**Gun emplacements**
**Route of attacking aircraft**

**Möhne Dam**

The attack routes taken by the crews to the various dams. This is the Möhne Dam

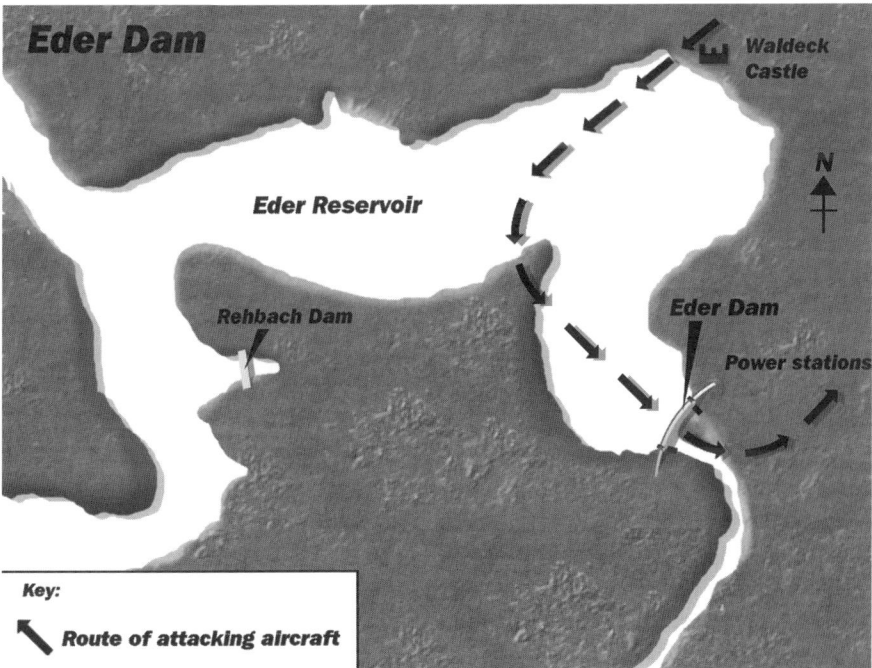

**Eder Dam**
**Waldeck Castle**
**N**
**Eder Reservoir**
**Rehbach Dam**
**Eder Dam**
**Power stations**

**Key:**
**Route of attacking aircraft**

Eder Dam

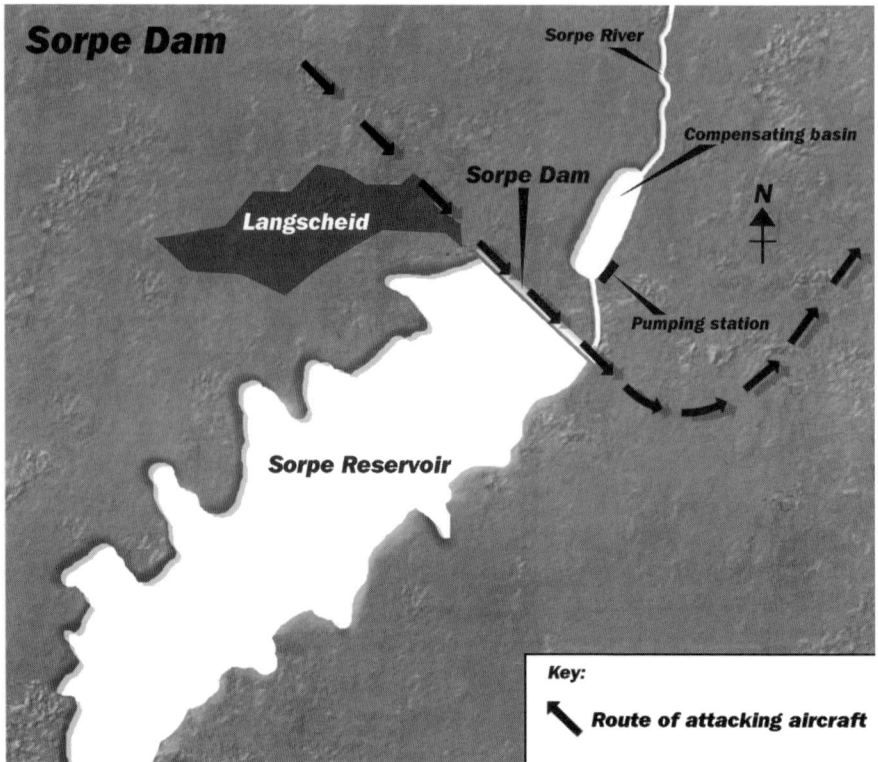

Sorpe Dam

On the evening of May 14th the Squadron's took off from Scampton for what would be the last exercise before 'Operation Chastise'. The crews were still unaware of the timing of the operation or their intended targets, but the atmosphere was subdued, with many anticipating that something significant would be happening in the near future. This time everything went according to plan. Gibson wrote in his logbook that this was a full dress rehearsal on Uppingham (Eyebrook) Lake and Colchester (Abberton) reservoir and that it had been completely successful.

On May 14 1943, the Chiefs of Staff in Washington signalled that the attack on the dams with 'Upkeep' should proceed, even though the anti-shipping weapon 'Highball' was not yet ready.

The following day, Bomber Command Headquarters were given the order for 'Operation Chastise' to proceed immediately, which was then passed to No. 5 Group Headquarters at Grantham. Air Vice-Marshal Cochrane travelled to Scampton to confirm that the operation would take place the following day. Returning to Grantham with Wing Commander Gibson, they reviewed the draft Operation Order and made last minute amendments. Back at Scampton early that evening, Gibson gathered his Flight Commanders, Squadron

Gibson (pipe in mouth) with his beloved pet Labrador '*Nigger*' who was killed in a traffic accident on the night of the 15th May

Leaders Young and Maudslay, together with Flight Lieutenants Hopgood and Hay for a discrete conference and informed them that they would be operating the next night.

As he left the meeting, Gibson was given the distressing news that his black Labrador, 'Nigger' had been hit by a car and killed outside Scampton's main gate. The young Wing Commander was deeply upset by the incident, but there was no time to mourn as he focussed on the task ahead. The following day, instructions were left for 'Nigger' to be buried at Scampton at midnight on the 16th, close to the time Gibson and the other waves of aircraft would be nearing their targets.

# CHAPTER SIX

# Operation 'Chastise'

The morning of Sunday 16th May began brightly. The sun shone as everybody on the apron at Scampton busied themselves for the day's activities. Except this was no ordinary day as 617 Squadron would be operating that night. No-one outside the Squadron was to know. Gibson instructed the Adjutant to draw up the Battle Order, to be labelled "Night Flying Programme" whilst armourers, fitters, riggers and other technicians prepared the aircraft for the night ahead. The final version of the Operation Order was typed and issued. Briefing for the crews began soon after mid-day when Gibson, accompanied by Wallis, revealed details of the forthcoming operation to aircraft Captains and Navigators. Meanwhile, the Wireless Operators were receiving their own specific instructions from No. 5 Group's Signals Officer, Wing Commander Dunn.

Later that afternoon, whilst crews were studying maps and photographs of their targets, aided by models of the Möhne and Sorpe reservoirs, Wallis and Mutt Summers, who had arrived at Scampton the previous day, moved between aircraft checking for the final time the condition of the weapons now firmly clamped between the calliper arms. Last minute panics were sorted out. The final briefing for all nineteen crews took place in the main briefing room in the early evening.

The tension was mounting. The walls were laden with identification posters and maps of Central Europe. Standing on a platform at the end of the room, accompanied by Wallis and Cochrane, Gibson stood statuesque, ready to address his crews. Calmly he began to explain that the attack was against the major dams of the Ruhr Valley.

He introduced Wallis, who described the principles behind 'Upkeep' and the importance of the dams to the German war economy. He was followed by Cochrane, who predicted the effects of a successful operation and emphasised the need to keep secret all aspects of the weapon, since it might well have future uses.

Gibson then re-iterated the plan of attack. The nineteen aircraft would depart from Scampton and fly at low altitude, just as they had practised for the last few weeks, in bright moonlight. The decision had been made to stag-

# Operation Chastise: The routes into Germany

Map depicting the outward journey to the Ruhr Valley

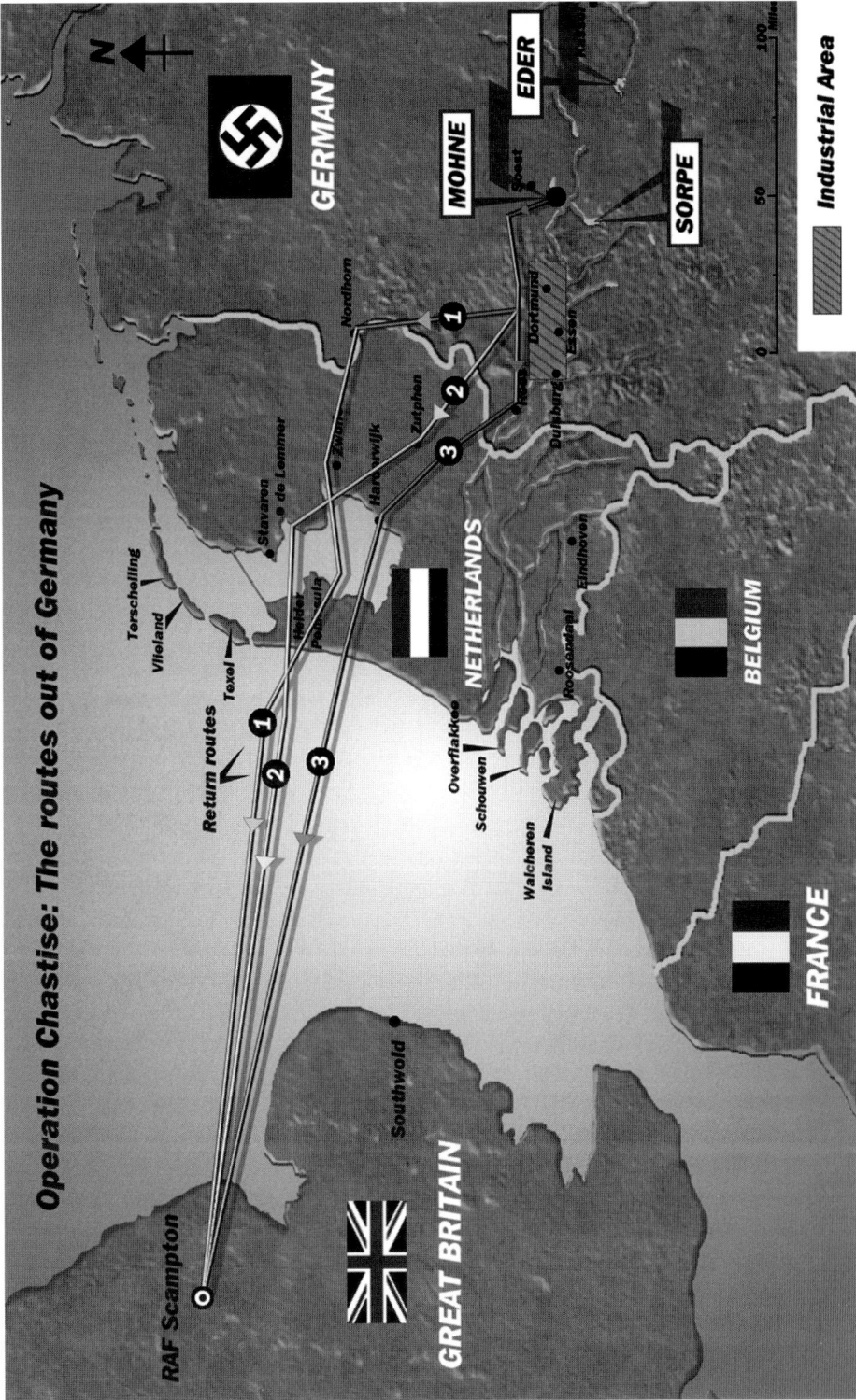

Map depicting the journey home and the areas where the crews were lost

ger the departure of the aircraft to allow for a period between attacks, so as not to congest the airspace around the targets, wasting valuable fuel and attracting unwanted attention from Luftwaffe night fighters.

Gibson himself would lead the attack. The first wave of aircraft would depart from Scampton at ten-minute intervals and consist of nine aircraft, divided into three equal groups. They would follow a southerly route to attack the Möhne Dam, code named 'Target X'. The aircraft would attack the target until there was a clear breach of the dam wall. Lancasters still carrying 'Upkeep' would continue to the Eder – 'Target Y'. Once the Eder had been breached, any remaining first wave aircraft with bombs would depart to the Sorpe –'Target Z'.

Flight Lieutenant Joe McCarthy would lead the second wave, consisting of five aircraft flying independently. These would fly to the Sorpe by a northerly route and would act as a diversionary force for the first group. As this route was slightly longer, they would take off before the first wave.

The remaining six aircraft would take off at one minute intervals shortly after midnight and cross the North Sea individually and following the same route as the first wave some two and a half hours before. This group would be a "mobile reserve", controlled directly by No. 5 Group Headquarters, to be detailed to attack targets that had not been breached by the first and second wave crews.

Pilots were briefed that they should not exceed a height of 1,500 feet above the English countryside and descend down to sixty feet over the North Sea. Their spotlights were to be used "for calibration" to avoid the danger of hitting the water. Approximately ten minutes from the target, it was decided that the three formation leaders, Gibson, Young and Maudslay should climb to 1000 feet in order to assess their position in relation to the target, before returning to low level. The crews should follow the progress of the attack on the VHF frequency, listening out for instructions, whilst spinning of the weapon should begin ten minutes before each aircraft was due to attack. The crews were briefed to attack their targets at an angle of ninety degrees, from sixty feet and at a ground speed of no more than 220 mph, using the triangulation bomb sight to determine the correct release point. Once the dam was destroyed, the remaining aircraft should plan a course for the next target. There was one notable variation. The attack against 'Target Z', the Sorpe Dam, would differ markedly from that against the other dams. Attacking aircraft were instructed to fly parallel to the dam at 180 mph, some 30 feet out over the lake and at the lowest practicable height. 'Upkeep' would not be spun, but dropped close to the wall near the centre of the target.

After the briefing, the crews retired for their customary pre-operational meal of two eggs and bacon followed by a brief rest period. Many composed last letters home to loved ones in case the unthinkable became reality.

The moment had arrived for the crews to collect their kit and be driven out to the dispersals ready to board their aircraft. The first man inside and in position was the Bomb Aimer, scrambling through the confines of the fuselage in full flying kit, to take up his position in the nose of the Lancaster. He was usually followed by the front Gunner, who sat directly above him in the front turret in control of two .303 Browning machine guns. Next aboard was the Pilot followed by the Flight Engineer, settling themselves into the cockpit, with the Navigator and the Wireless Operator seated at their positions behind them. The last man into the aircraft was the remaining Gunner, who entered the aircraft to take his position behind four Browning .303's in the rear turret.

A few minutes after nine o'clock, a very red light, signalled the aircraft designated to form the first wave, to start engines and taxi to the take off position. Approximately thirty minutes later, a green lamp flashed by the runway controller saw the first aircraft awkwardly begin its journey down the long grass runway at Scampton, gaining just enough speed to lift itself and its cumbersome load into the air and just clearing the boundary hedge. The first aircraft to depart should have been that of the American Joe McCarthy, but his own Lancaster was found to be unserviceable and the reserve had a missing compass card. As if these incidents were not enough, an accident saw his parachute rip-cord pulled, all of which delayed his take off by half an hour. As a result, it was Flight Lieutenant Barlow's crew who had the honour of launching one of the most illustrious nights in the Royal Air Force's history. New Zealander Flight Lieutenant Les Munro proceeded directly afterward, followed by Pilot Officers Byers and Rice. Their objective was the Sorpe Dam. Eight minutes later, Gibson led Flight Lieutenants Hopgood and Martin, the first aircraft of the second wave, down the runway and across the English countryside towards the Lincolnshire coastline. Shortly after 9.45pm, Squadron Leader Young departed, leading Flight Lieutenants Maltby and Shannon. Twelve minutes later, the last of the first wave departed with Squadron Leader Maudslay leading Flight Lieutenant Astell and Pilot Officer Knight. Flying in loose formation the aircraft settled down at little more than tree top level to cross the flat fenlands of East Anglia, heading for the North Sea and the Dutch coast.

Arrival over the Dutch coast was a little late and slightly off course due to a stronger wind than forecast. The problem was rectified immediately and the crews were back on track. The arrival of the first wave coincided with that of the second, but at different locations on the Dutch coast. This point also saw the first casualties of the mission. Some one and a half hours into his flight, Canadian Pilot Officer Vernon Byers' aircraft was hit by enemy flak crossing the Friesian island of Texel. They were higher than briefed at 300 feet and crashed into the Ijssel Meer. Only the body of Canadian Rear Gunner, Sergeant James McDowell was washed ashore by the strong currents, his body was recovered and buried in Harlingen. The remainder of the crew, Pilot Officer Vernon Byers, Sergeant Alastair Taylor, Flying Officer James Warner, Pilot Officer Arthur Whitaker, Sergeant John Wilkinson and Sergeant Charles Jarvie are commemorated at the Allied Air Forces Memorial at Runnymede, near Windsor. Pilot Officer Rice, following a minute or so behind Byers saw the explosion in the distance and almost became the second casualty of the night himself. Reducing altitude, his Lancaster sank toward the calm surface of the Ijssel Meer, the crew, were suddenly shaken by a violent jolt as the aircraft briefly made contact with water. Rice instinctively pulled back on the control column and the aircraft bounced into the air. When they had recovered from the shock and assessed the damage sustained by their aircraft they discovered that the impact had ripped the bomb from the underside of the Lancaster and with it ended their mission. With little alternative, Rice turned the aircraft and set course for Scampton. At almost the same time as Rice hit the water, Munro was in trouble. Having just crossed the island of Vlieland he

'Bomber' Harris and Air-Vice Marshal Robert Saundby discuss 'Operation Chastise'

was also hit by flak, fired either from an unseen flak ship or more likely by the island's defences. In the resultant burst of fire, one shell hit the aircraft severely damaging the compass, VHF radio and the communication system aboard the aircraft. This meant not only was navigation going to be an almost impossible task but the crew would not be able to communicate with the rest of the Squadron or amongst themselves. With little chance of success, it was decided to abort the mission and return to base at Scampton. There were now only two aircraft left of the five originally detailed to attack the Sorpe.

Led by Gibson's formation, the first wave had now crossed the enemy coast and was over Holland, picking their way through the known defences. Opposition was slight until they had crossed the Rhine but whilst passing around the northern edge of the Ruhr the formation flew into an unexpected defensive position. Searchlights illuminated the aircraft and light flak opened. The aircraft gunners opened up, targeting and extinguishing the searchlights but not before the German fire had damaged the wing of Hopgood's aircraft and injured several members of the crew. Despite bleeding from a head wound, Hopgood maintained formation and continued onward towards the Möhne Dam. In Gibson's aircraft his wireless operator sent a message back to No 5 Group warning the following aircraft to avoid these defences. In order to avoid any further flak positions the decision was taken to reduce height further and fly in close proximity to the flat countryside. The new height, combined with their speed, required greater levels of concentration from the crews as it was often necessary to deviate around church steeples and fly underneath high tension cables.

The second group of the first wave, led by Young was flying eight minutes behind Gibson. Shortly after crossing the coast they encountered flak near the town of Roosendaal but escaped unscathed. The formation would reach the Möhne Dam without loss. The final group of the first wave, led by Maudslay would not be as fortunate. There are two versions of the loss of Astells aircraft. The first was North of the Ruhr, South-West of the town of Borkum, Flight Lieutenant Astell's aircraft crashed after colliding with an electricity pylon, killing all on board. However it is also said that shortly before the turning point at the River Rhine, near the town of Rees, Astell, unsure of his position, tried to find a landmark by increasing their altitude slightly. This was a major error. Flak positions, which had targeted Gibson some moments earlier, quickly illuminated the sole aircraft in the night sky and although Sergeants Garbas and Bolitho in the front and rear turrets respectively, returned fire on the ground positions, the aircraft was soon enveloped in a crossfire that brought the Lancaster down in flames, killing all seven aboard. The first wave arrived at the Möhne reduced to eight aircraft.

Meanwhile, away to the north, the second wave detailed for the 'Sorpe' had suffered further losses. The demise of Byers and the forced return of Rice and

Lancaster preparing for take off

Munro had left only Barlow and the delayed McCarthy, who was speedily navigating towards his target, having cured the problems that had dogged him on the runway at Scampton.   As Flight Lieutenant Barlow and his crew crossed into German territory they collided with a high-tension cable crossing their path.   The aircraft crashed and exploded, killing all the crew, although by a quirk of fate the Upkeep it was carrying failed to detonate, providing the Germans with an intact weapon for inspection and analysis.   Now only McCarthy remained of the five, threading his way through the defences to the Sorpe Dam.

Gibson and the first wave of three aircraft had reached their destination and the aircraft familiarised themselves with the target area.   The wall of the Möhne Dam seemed impregnable.   Gibson flew a single reconnaissance operation over the dam in order to gauge the defences and confirm his plan of attack.   Meanwhile the other aircraft were arriving and circling low further down the lake, away from the defences.   The Intelligence report that there would be few guns was accurate, but three of these were on the dam wall, ideally positioned to offer fierce resistance to any aircraft flying in low across the water.

Gibson called up the other aircraft announcing that he was about to start his attack and that they should be ready to come in when they heard his instructions.   Unaware of the damage sustained by his deputy, Gibson reminded Hopgood that he was to assume control of the operation should he be shot down before the operation was completed.   The spotlights were switched on and Gibson brought the Lancaster down to the required height of 60 feet, levelling out at 230 mph with Upkeep spinning at 500 rpm.   The dam's defenders opened fire and as they came within range Gibson's Front Gunner John Deering opened up with a hail from his .303 Browning machine guns.   All the aircraft had been loaded with 100% tracer ammunition, producing the effect of a stream of continuous fire to unnerve the defenders.   When the towers on the dam aligned with the marks on his sight Flying Officer Spafford pressed the release. From the Rear Gunner position in the tail of the aircraft, Richard Trevor-Roper watched as Wallis' weapon skipped across the water towards its target.   After a short delay the surface of the lake erupted, water pouring over the dam. Those in a position to see thought that the dam had gone, but as the water calmed down it was seen to be still there.   Hutchison, the Wireless Operator conveyed the disappointing news via a coded message in Morse back to Headquarters at Grantham where Wallis, Cochrane and Harris eagerly awaited the news of the raid.   The short message 'Goner 68A' signified that the bomb had been successfully released but a breach had not occurred.

Some ten minutes elapsed whilst the remaining aircraft waited for the water to subside and the mist created by the explosion to dissipate.   The next to make his attack was Hopgood.   After circling the target patiently, the young pilot approached the target.   Now fully aware of the direction of attack, the

German Gunners on the towers were ready and waiting, opening up on Hopgood the moment he came within range with a volley of fire directly into his flight path. The aircraft was hit for a second time, quickly followed by multiple strikes that caused serious damage to the aircraft, setting it on fire engulfing the Lancaster in a ball of flame. The weapon was released late and bounced over the wall into the valley below, landing on the powerhouse located at the foot of the dam. Hopgood's aircraft struggled to gain height, two of the crew managed to escape from the stricken aircraft before it exploded in mid air and crashed into nearby open fields. The two survivors were the Bomb Aimer John Fraser and the Rear Gunner Tony Burcher, the latter sustaining serious injuries, offered no resistance when confronted with capture. Both were taken prisoner by the German authorities. After interrogation both men were transported to the notorious Stalag Luft III camp until their liberation at the conclusion of the war.

A third attack was now under way as Flight Lieutenant Martin commenced his approach. Showing little concern for his own safety, Gibson flew in ahead and to the right of the attacking aircraft drawing anti aircraft fire away from Martin providing him with a much clearer run at the target. Despite this Martin's aircraft was hit by flak but only sustained relatively slight damage. The mine was released and gambolled toward the target With smoke from Hopgood's bomb hampering his aim Flight Lieutenant Hay released his Upkeep. Following the pattern of some of those dropped in trials at Reculver the weapon veered off to the left, exploding away from the dam wall, causing no structural damage, but putting the flak gun on the left hand tower out of action. The appropriate signal was sent by Martin's Wireless Operator Leonard Chambers 'Goner 58A'. This was received a few minutes later and deciphered, creating growing anxiety in the Operations Room at Grantham. Three attacks had now failed to cause the desired effect. The dam still remained intact.

Gibson called in Squadron Leader Young to make the fourth attack. With Gibson and Martin acting as decoys, Young was able to approach the dam, reduce height to sixty feet and release his weapon with little opposition. Pulling up away from the target area Young and his crew watched the bomb skip several times across the surface of the water and sink in contact with the dam wall as Wallis had planned. This perfect, 'text-book' delivery would surely breach the structure. The vast column of water that rose after the explosion led to scenes of great expectancy on board the aircraft. This would be short lived, as once again the damage seemed to have been minimal. Reluctantly, the message 'Goner 78A' was released by the Wireless Operator Sergeant Nichols.

The fifth Lancaster waited for the effects of Young's detonation to subside. Visibility was perfect as Flight Lieutenant Maltby approached the spit of land that marked the start of the attack run. Lining up on the target and juggling

It took four attempts to destroy the Möhne Dam. Young's aircrew was credited with the breach on the fifth attempt

617 under heavy fire from anti-aircraft fire

his height and approach speed Maltby saw that the area in which Young had struck the wall was seriously damaged and water was starting to flow through a small breach near to the centre of the dam. Continuing his attack Maltby turned a little to port and released his mine which bounced four times before striking the dam. Again there was the tremendous column of water then the centre of the dam shattered, releasing a jet through a narrow breach that quickly disintegrated to form a massive hole unleashing a raging torrent. Inexplicably Sergeant Stone, Maltby's Wireless Operator sent an initial message stating that the dam was still intact, but this was soon succeeded by a message from Gibson's Wireless Operator containing one single code word that Headquarters had been waiting for. Long before the Morse had been fully translated it was clear that the incoming cipher spelt 'Nigger'. Grantham erupted. The mission to destroy the Möhne had been achieved.

With the Möhne Dam destroyed aircraft from the first wave still carrying Upkeep, led by Gibson and accompanied by Young set course for the Eder, approximately twenty minutes flying time away. Meanwhile Martin and Maltby, headed back to Scampton.

The return journey to Scampton was largely uneventful for Maltby. Apart from a little unwelcome hostility north of the Ruhr and from a defensive position on the southern tip of Texel, the aircraft landed safely at base, just after three o'clock. A little way behind Maltby, Martin flew on the same designated return route from the Möhne. After landing safely, the damage the plane suffered whilst attacking the Möhne became evident, a ruptured fuel tank, which fortunately, had been drained before it was struck, and had damaged an aileron on the starboard wing. Out of the nineteen aircraft despatched four were now safely back at Scampton.

Gibson led the five remaining Lancasters towards the Eder. Maudslay and Shannon still carried their Upkeep. At the time of the breach at the Möhne, Shannon had been lining up for his own attack and was ordered to abort when it was clear that the combined efforts of Young and Maltby had been successful. Young was now in place to lead operations should anything disastrous happen to Gibson.

At Scampton the reserve formation had taken off shortly after midnight and was heading into enemy territory awaiting instructions from 5 Group Headquarters as to which dam to attack. Pilot Officer Lewis Burpee would lead the reserve team off from Scampton. Flying independently of each other, the four remaining Lancasters were now on an operation to attack any of the primary dams that had failed to be breached by the first two waves, with the objective of ensuring that they were destroyed. At the same time, McCarthy, the sole survivor of the aircrews which left on the second wave to attack the Sorpe, was nearing the objective of his journey having engaged and evaded hostile defences along his route. The Sorpe Dam was shrouded in mist and was impossible to find initially until a small break in the dense cloud allowed him to determine the exact location of his target. The attack run did not go according to plan. Unlike the Möhne and the Eder which were gravity dams, Wallis believed that in order to breach the concrete core of the dam, up to five 'Upkeep' mines would have to be utilised. The Sorpe was an earth dam and required a different method of attack. The intention was to drop the mines in order to weaken the concrete core and allow the resulting water seepage to ultimately undermine the structure causing it to implode. Although the dam itself was not defended, it proved a difficult approach due to the rolling steep hills and a church spire right in line with the bombing run along the length of the dam. A series of aborted approaches followed.

Unaware that his was the sole surviving aircraft to attack the Sorpe, McCarthy exercised incredible skill and patience in order to get the approach and release of the weapon absolutely perfect. His task was to release his mine so subsequent attacks by others would lead to the dams demise. In all, McCarthy approached and aborted his attack on nine occasions. The Bomb Aimer, Sergeant George Johnson repeatedly called for McCarthy to abort the run at the last minute unhappy about the height of the aircraft or the line of approach. Many of the crew were becoming restless, so on the tenth run at a height of only thirty feet, judged without the aid of spotlights, the bomb was released which exploded in the water near to the centre of the dam. Nearly twenty feet of the crest had crumbled but this in itself was not enough to force the dam to disintegrate as hoped. Inexplicably the message that the bomb had been released did not reach headquarters at Grantham until very near the end of the return journey to Scampton.

The Wireless Operator Leonard Eaton used Morse code to signal 'Goner 79C' indicating that the bomb had indeed been successfully released and that a minor breach had occurred. The return journey, which should have been straightforward, proved very much otherwise. Due to compass problems, McCarthy consistently found himself off course and entering dangerous, well-defended areas. Having survived crossing the heavily defended marshalling yards near Hamm, McCarthy managed to plot a course which would at least get the crew home crossing the Zuider Zee on the Dutch coast and continuing in a westerly direction towards base. As the aircraft's undercarriage touched the grass of the runway at Scampton, the aircraft lurched and sank to the right hand side. The starboard wheel had been pierced by enemy fire and went unnoticed by the crew until a rude awakening in Lincolnshire. Fortunately for the remaining crew, their pilot expertly countered the puncture to bring the aircraft to a safe halt inside the airfield perimeter.

The five aircraft of the first wave had traversed the hilly countryside between the Möhne and the Eder and were approaching their target. Gibson had made a slight navigational error, but found the dam which was shrouded

The deadly mission into enemy territory

in a thick mist. Gibson's would not be the only crew which found locating the dam difficult. As each crew independently navigated toward the new target with no radio contact to help them align with each other, they found themselves slightly and inadvertently off course, which only became evident when they reached the Eder reservoir a few miles west of where the actual dam stood. Mist filling the valleys made it difficult to identify the target. The mist made each valley look as though it could possibly contain a lake so each had to be navigated as a process of elimination. Gibson found it and summoned the others by firing very cartridges over the dam. Fortunately, unlike the Möhne, the Eder Dam was undefended apart from a company of riflemen, designed to halt any attempt by saboteurs to attack the dam (such as the Special Operations Executive (SOE) or paratroops) and certainly no threat to the aircrews.

With the target located Gibson ordered the first of the attacks against the Eder. Flight Lieutenant David Shannon, who had been due to release his weapon at the Möhne but was told to abort after the dam was breached, made the first attempt. Despite the lack of defences the approach to the Eder was far more difficult than that at the Möhne. The major problem that Shannon and the rest of the remaining crews faced was that the approach to the target was extremely difficult, it was surrounded on all sides by steep hills and a spit of land jutted into the lake ahead of the dam. In order to attack the dam, the

Nineteen Lancasters participated on Operation Chastise, only 11 returned

pilots would have to fly the aircraft over Waldeck Castle situated on top of a hill and make a steep dive of nearly 1,000 feet to the valley below and make a sharp turn to port before adjusting the Lancaster to the appropriate attack height and speed. There was a very short time before the release point was reached. Immediately after this full power was required and a steep turn to starboard in order to clear rising ground beyond the dam. After several attempts Shannon still had been unable to make a correct approach on the target. Telling him to hold off, Gibson called up Squadron Leader Maudslay for an attempt. Maudslay made two unsuccessful attempts before Shannon tried again. Finally, after two more runs Shannon approached at the correct height and airspeed, then releasing his Upkeep at exactly the right place. The mine sped towards the target bouncing a number of times before striking the dam a little right of centre and sinking beneath the surface before exploding, sending the familiar waterspout high into the bright moonlit sky. Shannon believed they had made a small breach and his Wireless Operator sent back the message, 'Goner 79B'. On closer inspection, after the surge had subsided, other observers saw there was no apparent breach to the dam.

The next to attempt the breach was Squadron Leader Henry Maudslay. Like Shannon, Maudslay had difficulty in perfecting the approach to the target. After two aborted runs the third appeared to be more successful. Gibson watched as the aircraft completed its final manoeuvre and approached the dam. Maudslay's aircraft may have been damaged, one witness reported seeing something, hanging down from the underside of the Lancaster as it made its approach. For whatever reason, Maudslay's Upkeep was released too close to the dam. It hit the crest with tremendous force and detonated instantly behind the aircraft. The damaged aircraft climbed and headed west in a vain attempt to reach safe territory. Gibson called Maudslay by VHF and received only a very weak reply. At the time it was thought that he had been destroyed by his own bomb, an interpretation perpetuated by several post war accounts, and the 'Dambusters' film. In fact Maudslay managed to control the plane and head back to Scampton only to be shot down by flak near the town of Emmerich a few miles short of the Dutch border near to Nijmegen with the total loss of its crew.

One aircraft still carrying its weapon remained to attack the Eder Dam. Pilot Officer Les Knight also had great difficulty in aligning the aircraft onto a correct line of approach after completing the steep descent from the castle. However, after one unsuccessful attempt that nearly saw the plane smash into the steep hill at the end of the bomb run, Knight approached the target again, this time successfully adjusting course and speed after the tricky descent. At the exact moment the weapon was released the aircraft climbed steeply away to safety. The crew watched in anticipation as the bomb sank in contact with the dam wall. The explosion that followed sent a massive plume of water into the sky. A small hole appeared about 30 feet beneath the crest which crumbled as the breach widened and a tidal wave swept down the steep valley. The jubilation was evident as the call sign 'Dinghy', signifying the breach of the dam, was sent back to Grantham. The jubilant crews still had to face the dangers of the return journey. David Shannon arrived back at Scampton unscathed after experiencing little opposition on the return journey, which followed the same route as Maltby and Martin less than one hour before. A single bullet hole was the sum of the damage inflicted upon Shannon's aircraft. Within ten minutes of Shannon's arrival, Wing Commander Gibson touched down. Following a different route from the preceding three aircraft, he landed at Scampton at just after four o'clock, Gibson's journey home had not been uneventful though. According to his account in his book "Enemy Coast Ahead" having returned to the Möhne to inspect the damage, Gibson had to drop extremely low to shake off the attentions of a fighter aircraft which the Rear Gunner Trevor-Roper had thought appeared on the horizon to the Lancaster's rear. If the fighter existed it did not engage the bomber at any point and the aircraft carried on unmolested. The next aircraft to land was that of Knight. Again the Lancaster was barely troubled on its return journey. Only a rogue flak position at the Möhne and several close calls around defended sites as the aircraft drifted off course caused any alarm to the crew. The threat of the deadly night fighter proved unfounded. The Lancaster touched down barely ten minutes behind Gibson and seven weary crew, flying for well over six hours left their positions in the aircraft and descended the crew ladder to terra firma. The jubilation of the crews as they met in the mess after landing was tempered by the knowledge that a number of crews would not be coming back. After flying as deputy leader to the Eder, Young flew back to the Möhne as briefed and returned across Germany and Holland via the third homeward route also used by Gibson. Crossing the Dutch coast and possibly flying a little too high, he was shot down by a naval flak battery and crashed into the sea with no survivors.

With no more aircraft available from the first and second waves, the signals were given by Group Headquarters for each of the reserve aircraft to divert to their targets. Group Headquarters directed those of the reserve force to their targets. Pilot Officer Warner Ottley was one of the first to acknowledge the signal, he was altering course for the Lister Dam. As they approached the city of Hamm they were slightly off track and the aircraft was caught in a bathe of searchlights and struck by intense anti-aircraft fire. The Lancaster fell from the sky and exploded as it ploughed into the ground killing all but one onboard. The sole survivor was the Rear Gunner Sergeant Tees who had been blown clear of the stricken aircraft as it exploded. Badly injured, he was captured by the authorities shortly afterwards. He was taken to hospital for treatment before being sent to camp L6 at Heydekruge.

Shortly before Ottley's demise Pilot Officer Burpee had also been shot down. Without realising his true position, Burpee had inadvertently flown directly

The bomb drop

Crews feared an attack on the Tirpitz was imminent. Gibson and other crewmembers were relieved to find out that in fact, it was a mission to destroy the Ruhr dam

over the heavily defended airfield at Gilze Rijn on their way to attack the Sorpe. The aircraft crashed onto the airfield and exploded. The force of the explosion ripped through administrative buildings and hangars, damaging aircraft and equipment. Canadian Flight Sergeant Ken Brown witnessed from a distance the demise of both Ottley and Burpee, crashing in a tremendous ball of flame. Flight Sergeant Townsend, following also saw Ottley go down. Gibson, flying near to Hamm whilst returning after completing his mission, reported seeing what he hoped was an enemy fighter destroyed by flak but it is more likely this was the unfortunate Ottley and his crew.

Brown was on route to the Sorpe to try to finish what McCarthy had begun hours earlier. Already Brown's crew had engaged trains en route and received hits from ground fire, one shot entering the fuselage but missing all vital components. Brown reached the Sorpe in the early hours and like McCarthy had trouble locating the dam. Once found, there were further problems with the approach. After nine unsuccessful attempts to attain the perfect approach, Brown succeeded in attacking at exactly the right height and speed. Like McCarthy's bomb, the explosion rocked the central core and caused further damage to the crest but failed to cause any appreciable breach. With the weapon successfully released and the message 'Goner 78C' transmitted back to Headquarters, Brown set course for home. This course took the aircraft in a north-westerly direction, deliberately flying over the damaged Möhne Dam. The crew reported significant breaches in the structure with a tremendous amount of water surging through the gaps and into the valley below, which now resembled a reservoir itself. However, the return journey was not yet complete and deep inside German territory, the aircrews were still vulnerable to anti-aircraft fire from now attentive defenders not far below them.

Near Hamm, where Ottley had been downed a few hours previously, Brown also came under attack His aircraft was fortunate to escape without damage. This was still enough to persuade Brown to opt for maximum throttle and a further reduction of altitude. As they were nearing the Dutch coast the aircraft was caught by searchlights and flak opened up on them, peppering the fuselage and cockpit canopy with holes. They were lucky and were out of range before anything vital was hit. The aircraft touched down at Scampton at just after five o'clock on the 17th May much to the relief of its exhausted crew.

Flight Sergeant Cyril Anderson had been instructed to attack the Sorpe Dam. However with a defective rear turret and compass problems which caused them to stray well off track they realised that their chances of success were slim. With only a short while until day would start to dawn Anderson turned the aircraft for home and the message was relayed that they had been unsuccessful by the Wireless Operator William Bickle. The crew landed back at Scampton in the early morning sunshine with the bomb still aboard.

The last of the reserve wave to attack was Flight Sergeant Bill Townsend. He was directed to attack the Ennepe Dam on the River Schwelme. The early morning mist was again proving a difficult proposition and making the target areas invisible until the aircraft passed extremely close. Seeing a dam which he believed to be the Ennepe he made three attempts to ensure that his one and only chance of destroying the target would be a success. Fortunately for Townsend, the dam had no defence and so his runs were completed without opposition. On his fourth run the bomb was released and sank some distance from the dam having bounced twice. There were however, no further aircraft on route to the site and the dam would remain undamaged. The signal 'Goner 58E' was sent back to Grantham informing them that the bomb had been released but there was no apparent sign of breaching. Townsend was the last aircraft to attack and would be the last to return from the raid. He landed in daylight just after six o'clock in the morning after a hair raising return journey through Germany and Holland, the latter part in daylight. To the crew's surprise, enemy fighters did not engage them and their speed and low height saved them from light flak. The only area that nearly proved their downfall near to the island of Texel which had already claimed the lives of Byers' crew on the outward journey. Indeed, the attention that they received from Texel made Townsend alter course to avoid further confrontation from the position. The new route briefly returned them towards enemy territory but offered them a much safer route back between the Dutch islands and across the North Sea. A faulty oil gauge would further hamper their return to Lincolnshire and force a decision to shut down the apparently offending engine. This was the last mishap of an eventful journey; the aircraft touched down on the grass runway and came to a standstill. All the aircraft that had survived the raid were now scattered unceremoniously across the wide expanse of Scampton. Eleven of the nineteen had returned safely, some unscathed, others with varying degrees of damage. As time passed it became apparent that eight aircraft would not be coming back.

---

[1] A certain amount of confusion surrounds the details of Astell's downfall Sweetman and other suggest, as I do, that this was as a result of enemy ground fire. However, Cooper has taken the viewpoint that the aircraft crashed after striking a low-level cable

The deadly attack

# CHAPTER SEVEN

# *Aftermath*

The morning of the 17th May 1943 saw the first of the successful aircrew return to their home base at Scampton.  It had been daylight for many hours as the last of the surviving crews were approaching the runway for landing.  Several of them, low on fuel or badly damaged simply touched down and rolled to a halt.  The crews disembarking at the first available opportunity leaving a scene of aircraft strewn across the airfield awaiting recovery by the ground crews.

Wallis waited patiently, even after the last aircraft had landed, he thought perhaps other crews had returned by longer routes to avoid detection, or the consumption of fuel meant that the last few miles would be completed at the lowest possible air speed.  The desire to see further crews arrive back in Lincolnshire was slowly overturned by the realisation that eight young air-

Calm in the skies prior to the attack

The mission was one of the first low altitude-bombing raids in history

crews had lost their lives on the mission. Like the surviving crews, the engineer was elated that the mission and the weapon had proved a massive success, but equally he mourned for those crews, which he incorrectly determined, he had sent to premature deaths.

Less than one hour after the last of the aircraft had touched down, a reconnaissance Spitfire took off to ascertain the extent of the damage. The morning light showed the damage to the dams and the extent to which the resulting floodwaters had battered the surrounding landscape. The photographic evidence it collected would have a tremendous morale boosting effect both at home and in occupied territory. It was also influential on Britain's allies. Churchill, who was in Washington addressing the US Congress, provided one of his most important and influential speeches. For fifty minutes, the British Prime Minister described the important and devastating blows to Germany, convincing the Americans that the allied offensive against Germany was having a marked effect, and encouraging them to maintain their forces in Europe, rather than concentrate solely on the war in the Pacific.

The letters and telegrams of congratulation began to flood in to those involved directly with the operation early on the 17th May. Amongst the first came a detailed telegram from Sir Archibald Sinclair, the Secretary of State for Air. The message, on behalf of the War Cabinet gleefully acknowledged the result of the Dams Raid and the subsequent damage to German industry and infrastructure. Harris received praise for the success of Bomber Command's raids against Germany. Cochrane sent special praise to the crews who had carried out the mission and the founder of the RAF Lord Trenchard praised the work of Bomber Command.

All the major newspapers contained news of the raid on their coveted front covers. The major broadsheets and popular press carried the triumphant news alongside the more traditional metropolitan and rural papers. All carried the first reconnaissance photographs of the giant Möhne Dam with the huge breach and water cascading into the valley below. The BBC broadcast the details of the raid using an official communiqué. They described the attack on the three major German dams, providing many with their first details of the raid.

Contrary to belief, the crews of 617 Squadron were not the only allied aircrews in the sky over Germany on the 16th May. There were also nine Mosquito aircraft bombing German cities and fifty four other aircraft, including Wellingtons performing mining operations, code named 'Gardening', over the North Sea area and the Bay of Biscay.

It was now evident that all the hours of hard work by Wallis, the initial rejection and then acceptance of his idea to destroy the German dams had been worthwhile. German industry had been dealt a blow, not perhaps the decisive war shortening episode that the planners had originally hoped for in the late 1930's, but damaging nonetheless. German war production in the

The bomb that would change the thinking of the Third Reich

Most of the planes cleared the dams without major problems

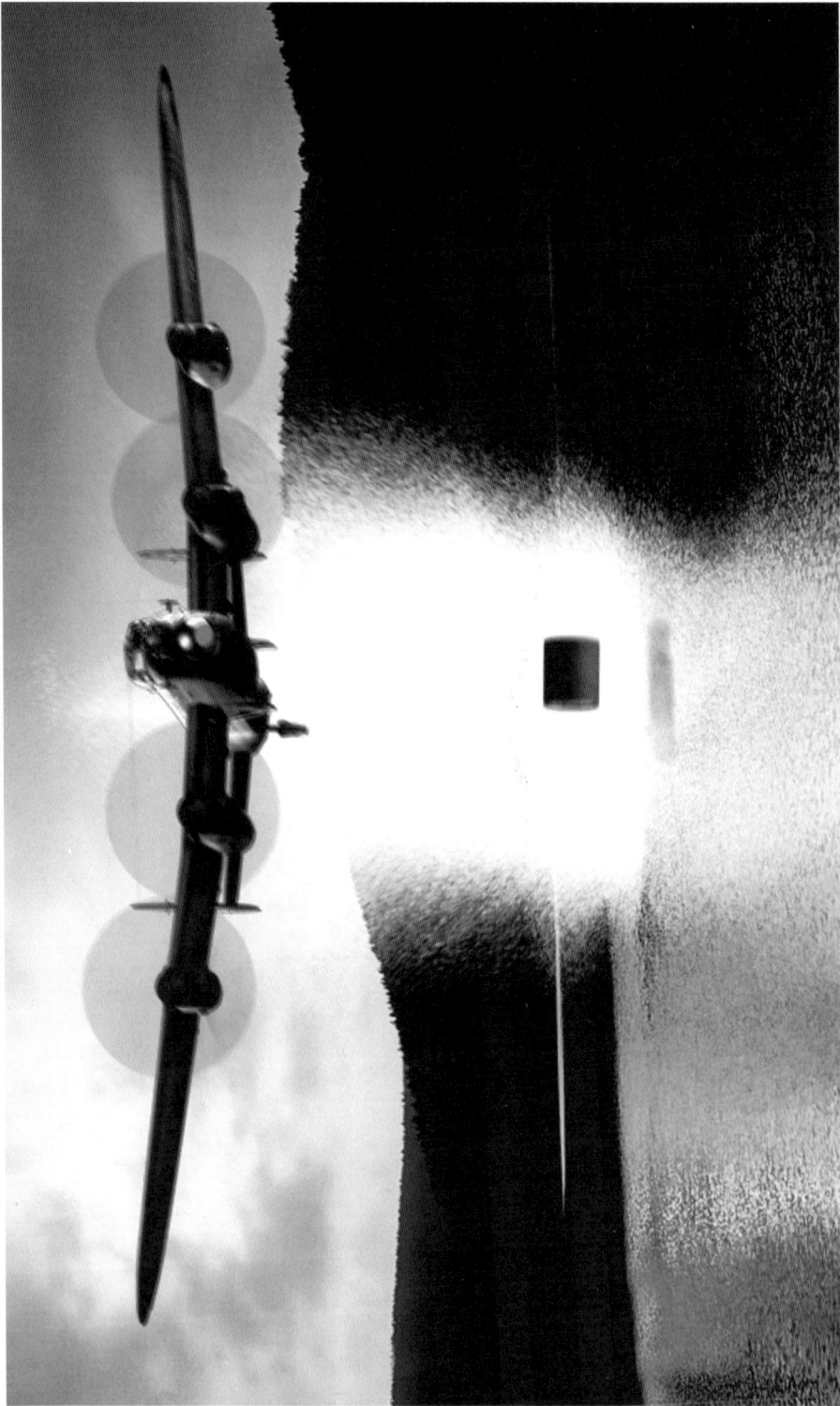

The attack on the Möhne

Ruhr was reduced. The domino effect took hold and for months after the event there were significant shortages of raw materials for the essential weapons that Germany needed to secure the Eastern front. The major industrial towns were flooded, some impassable for days, railways were swept away

Ariel view of the Möhne after the breach

and it was evident that the repair would cause more economic constraints on the Third Reich and force it to relocate troops and workers from other important projects in order to complete the reconstruction. There was now a severe water shortage in the Ruhr and for a time strict rationing would have to be implemented. The important waterworks that supplied heavily industrialised areas were out of commission for months and not fully restored until August, a significant period for the loss of important industrial supplies. In Neheim, for example, only essential supplies were reconnected. The steel industry of the Ruhr area, seriously affected by the effects of the Dams Raid saw a further decrease in its manufacturing output due to the damage caused by further Allied raids on the region. Coking plants, starved of water, were particularly badly affected, depriving industry of vital fuel. The loss not only decreased production of manufactured goods, it also caused a substantial rationing pro-

Aerial view of the Eder after the breach

Front view of the Eder

gramme to be adopted as gas supplies were dramatically reduced, in some cases by as much as sixty per cent.

The dams may have been breached, but they were not totally destroyed. Hundreds of workers were diverted from other essential war work, including the Atlantic Wall defences to assist with reconstruction. The Möhne was repaired by September 1943 and the Eder by the following month, ready for the winter rains that would refill the reservoirs. The raid was a terrible blow upon arable agriculture and livestock farming in the area. The loss of hundreds of cattle and pigs would have a serious detrimental affect alone. The sudden decline in livestock meant an immediate rationing of meat and dairy products. However, in addition to this, thousands of acres of rich farm land were damaged by a thick layer of silt which had replaced the top soil.

Perhaps one of the biggest changes produced by the bombing was the drastic psychological effect that saw the military increase defences across Germany, especially at reservoirs. In addition to extra torpedo nets, which had proved inadequate during the attack anyway, the authorities also installed deflector nets and poles and reduced the water capacity of the reservoirs. These additional defences made great demands upon manpower. In all, it could be expected that a substantial number of personnel could be tied up protecting a site that might, or might not be attacked.

The effect on German civilians was evident. Despite attempts to reassure the population and play down the effects of the raid there was increased concern about the Allies' ability to attack important targets with devastating effect. The failings of the Luftwaffe had been highlighted and the arrogance of the leadership had been exposed. The Allies, unsurprisingly, saw the raid as a massive propaganda coup. The newspaper and radio coverage came at a good time and offered the population of Britain, many of whom had suffered tremendously in the Blitz, with new hope. The post raid photographs provided tangible evidence that the raid had been successful and the German war machine was vulnerable to attack by Allied aircraft. The morale of the nation had been visibly lifted. The morale of others was lifted also, especially those who were detained in prison camps, now given encouragement that the war my soon be over and that their liberation was close.

The Allies around the world reacted with great support and praise for the operation. The most heartfelt congratulations on the success of the operation came from the Dutch who had suffered terribly since they were invaded and occupied during the Blitzkrieg. In other occupied regions, the RAF wasted very little time or opportunity to herald the news of their success against the Germans in their own backyard. Many major French Cities, including Toulouse, were subjected to a major propaganda exercise, which involved the dropping of simple leaflets proclaiming the success and showing the dams before and after the raid, utilising the reconnaissance photographs taken hours after the attack.

Millions of gallons of water poured into the Ruhr Valley

The leaflets provided the pockets of French Resistance with a belief that they could defeat the Germans, whilst serving notice on the Vichy and other Officials that their dominance was waning. In Washington, the response was enthusiastic and for the first time during the war the use of bombers could be recognised as a legitimate weapon in the bid to oust the German leadership. The Russians, so frequently quick to criticise Churchill and Roosevelt for their lack of ambition against the Reich in Occupied Europe, spoke openly of their admiration for the British offensive against the dams. The Russians continued with a request for information about the project as they had been so impressed by its daring and effectiveness, that they had begun to consider a similar weapon which their Navy could utilise against the Germans. Reservations in London soon turned to opportunism. Initially fearing a leak of secret information and the threat that a similar weapon would pose to British shipping in the future should the alliance turn sour, the Ministry had been reluctant to release details of the project. However, after much consideration, it was felt that the plans for 'Upkeep' were different to those of 'Highball'. A definite increase in Anglo-Soviet relations would result from the information exchange and the RAF would receive a boost of its prestige around the world. With this in mind it was decided to pass the relevant information to the Soviets.

The immense flood of water through the Möhne Dam

The consequences of the raid had significant implications both in Washington and at home, but not everything had gone according to plan that night. In particular, the Sorpe Dam, considered by some to be complementary to the Möhne, had not been breached. The damage that would have been caused had the Sorpe Dam also collapsed is a point of great contention, but one that will never be fully answered.

Of the original 19 aircraft only 11 returned, 53 crewmembers were dead. The Canadian Sergeant Vernon Byers piloted the first lost aircraft. Having left Scampton as part of the second group he had reached the Dutch coast at approximately eleven o'clock. The heavily defended island of Texel stood directly in his flight path and the ferocious anti-aircraft volley from the ground saw Byers hit and crashing into the sea. The height at which the aircraft was hit, just 300 feet above the surface of the water gave Byers little time to react once his aircraft had been hit. All the other members of the Lancaster ED934 AK-J, Flight Engineer, Sergeant Alastair Taylor who had completed only four missions, Pilot Officer James Warner the Navigator, Bomb Aimer Sergeant Neville Whittaker, Wireless Operator Sergeant John Wilkinson and the two Gunners, Sergeant Charles Jarvie and Sergeant James McDowell, died as a result of crashing into the Issel Meer. Only the body of McDowell was recovered and he was buried in the Harlingen General Cemetery in Holland. The rest of the crew is commemorated on the Memorial at Runnymede.

The second aircraft to be lost was piloted by Flight Lieutenant Astell DFC. He died instantly when his Lancaster ED864 AJ-B, whilst flying at low altitude, struck a high-tension power cable directly in its path. There were no survivors. Sergeant Kinnear, Pilot Officer Wile, Flying Officer Hopkinson, and Sergeants Garshowitz, Garbas and Bolitho were recovered and are now buried in the Reichswald Forest War Cemetery, five kilometres South West of Kleve.

The third aircraft lost on the raid was that of the Australian, Flight Lieutenant Barlow DFC. Barlow and the crew of ED927 AJ-E perished in similar circumstances to Astell on their way to target the Sorpe Dam, after hitting a power cable, which was unseen in their vision directly on their flight path. Barlow's body was recovered from the crash scene along with the other six members of the crew, Pilot Officer Whillis, Flying Officer Burgess, Pilot Officer Gillespie DFM, Flying Officer Williams DFC, Flying Officer Glinz and Sergeant Liddell, who had all died instantly. They were taken to the Reichswald Forest War Cemetery near Kleve, having being originally buried in local a local cemetery during the War, then re-interred in the post war period. The fourth aircraft to be destroyed in action, ED925 AJ-M, was piloted by Flight Lieutenant Hopgood DFC Bar. It was the second aircraft to attack the dam. Whilst approaching the Möhne Dam, Hopgood's aircraft was caught be flak situated on the sluice towers. The weapon was released slightly too late and the subsequent explosion caused irreparable damage to the aircraft. Hopood bravely wrestled with the controls giving enough time for two crewmembers to leave the aircraft before it plunged in flames and exploded nearby. All but two of the crew perished. Along with Hopgood, Sergeant Brennan, the Flight Engineer, Flying Officer Earnshaw the Navigator, Sergeant Minchin the Radio Operator and Pilot Officer Gregory DFM all lost their lives. They are buried in the Rheinberg War Cemetery near Wesel. The two survivors jettisoned from the aircraft were the Bomb Aimer Pilot Officer Fraser and the Rear Gunner Pilot Officer Burcher. Both were captured after sustaining severe injuries and spent the war as captives at the notorious Stalag Luft III camp. A stone now marks the spot where the aircraft crashed.

Pilot Officer Burpee DFM flew ED865 AJ-S. The Canadian had left Scampton just after midnight and had strayed slightly off course due to being unable to clarify exact position from low altitude. They were downed by flak near Gilze Rijn airfield in Holland. All the crew were killed. The other six members were Sergeants Jaye, Pegler, Arthur and Long, along with Pilot Officer Weller and Flight Sergeant Brady. With an average age of just 23, this was one of the youngest crews to take part in the raid. The entire crew is now buried in Bergen op Zoom Cemetery.

Pilot Officer Ottley DFC flew the sixth aircraft lost ED910 AJ-C. It was due to launch its 'Upkeep' mine against the Lister Dam but was hit by flak whilst en-route. The aircraft crashed near Hamm at half past two in the morning of the 17th May. All but one of the crew perished. The lone survivor was Sergeant Tees who was badly injured and captured shortly afterwards. A symbolic cross now marks the position where the aircraft crashed. Along with Ottley, the crash also claimed the lives of Sergeants Strange, Marsden, Guterman DFM, Flight Sergeant Johnston and Flying Officer Barrett. All are now buried in Reichswald Forest War Cemetery.

The seventh crew lost was that piloted by the Old Etonian, Squadron Leader Henry Maudslay DFC. His aircraft ED934 AJ-K had left Scampton and was flown into Germany to target the Eder Dam. After making several trial runs Maudslay finally dispatched the 'Upkeep' mine. This was, unfortunately, slightly too late and the mine bounced over the parapet of the dam. The explosion seriously damaged Maudslay's aircraft and as a result the flight home was complicated. Just inside German territory, his aircraft was struck by flak and crashed. Along with Maudslay, the RAF also lost the lives of six other crewmembers. These were Sergeants Marriott DFM and Burrows, Flight Officers Urquhart DFC and Tytherleigh DFC, Pilot Officer Fuller and Warrant Officer Cottam. Their bodies were recovered and initially they were buried at the Nordfreidhof near Dusseldorf, but after the war were exhumed and reburied near their colleagues from the raid in Reichswald Forest War Cemetery.

The final crew too be lost during the raid on the German dams was that of the Lancaster ED887 AJ-A. Flown by Squadron Leader Henry 'Dinghy' Young DFC Bar, released their 'Upkeep' mine against the Möhne Dam. They then flew as support for aircraft attacking the Eder after the Möhne had been breached. The crew was returning over the Dutch coast on the final leg of the mission when a German coastal defence unit targeted them. The aircraft sustained damage and crashed off the coast. The crew consisting of Squadron Leader Young, Sergeant s Horsfall, Nichols, Yeo and Ibbotson, Flying Officer McCausland and Flight Sergeant Roberts perished at just before three o'clock in the morning. Their bodies were washed ashore and taken for burial in Bergen General Cemetery, Holland.

The total number of lives lost that night was fifty-four. Only three members of the eight crews lost survived as Prisoners of War. This amounted to a loss rate of over forty-percent. Most of those who survived the raid would continue to fly operations with 617 Squadron, with at least another thirty losing their lives in accidents or subsequent operations with 617 Squadron or other units. Many of those who survived the Dams Raid lost their lives just four short months later in a disastrous attack on the Dortmund-Ems Canal. Wing Commander Gibson, whose skill and bravery contributed much to the success of the operation would not survive the war. After a lengthy absence from flying operations for the RAF (during which he was sent on a morale boosting tour of the USA and Canada as an envoy of Churchill) Gibson became a staff officer, technically a ground job, although he still managed to fly on a few operations. The last of these was on the 19th September 1944, when he appointed himself as Master Bomber and flew in a Mosquito on a raid on München Gladbach and Rheydt. After directing the bombing he was heard leaving the target area but his aircraft crashed at Steenbergen -en-Kruisland in Holland on the return flight. The cause of his crash has never been fully determined, although evidence suggests that he may have run out of fuel or suffered a mechanical failure. His remains and those of his navigator Squadron Leader James Warwick are buried in the local cemetery in Steenbergen. Gibson was only 26.

CHAPTER EIGHT

# Die Nachwirkung
## The Aftermath – from the German Perspective

O n the morning of the 17th May 1943, the Minister of Munitions, Dr Albert Speer, personal confidant and friend of Adolf Hitler, arrived by plane to the scene of devastation that had materialised in the hours since the breaching of the dams.

After landing at Werl, some distance away, but the closest available airstrip to the devastation at the Möhne, he was informed that villages, towns and cities were affected over a massive geographical area. Speer could see the damage to the Möhne for himself. A breach, partly from the initial destructive explosion, but now greatly expanded by the sheer force of the water spewing from the gaping hole.

Approximately seventy-six meters wide and twenty-two meters deep, the breach in the Möhne had expelled 116 million cubic meters of water in twelve hours. Such was Speer's initial shock at what he saw, he immediately ordered an immediate increase in aerial defence for all the sensitive targets in Germany. The anti-torpedo nets had been ripped away from their moorings and lay beached upon the far side of the compensating basin below the dam. A twenty-ton turbine from the decimated plant had been picked up and swept a hundred meters downstream.

The torrent that flowed through the narrow valley caused massive damage to the towns in its path. The maelstrom that ripped along at speeds of fifteen to twenty miles per hour tore up houses, bridges, railways and roads. Only people fortunate enough to live on higher ground were not affected. The tidal wave, approximately ten meters high, extended as far as sixty-five kilometres away before water levels returned to normal and conurbations no longer had badly flooded streets. Surveyors and engineers reported damage to important bridges and viaducts as far away as fifty kilometres. Within six hours of the breach, the surge had reached the Ruhr, directly fed from the Möhne and 150 kilometres away from the dam.

Witness reports provide a perspective on the raid from the viewpoint of the population of the valleys in the vacinity of the dams. The vividness of the attack still haunted many of those interviewed for witness statements, even

Flying over the dam

Low flying to avoid flak and detection

Gibson explains to King George VI how the Germans were dealt such a deadly blow

though they were not collated until October 1945, almost two and a half years after the attack took place.

The events of the night of 16th May 1943 began, according to the witnesses, quietly. Then around 11.30pm, the wailing scream of the siren began. A small number of aircraft, reports suggested four, flew over the town of Soest some time later and on toward the Möhne Dam. This number is incorrect however, as the timing indicates the arrival was that of the first wave of aircraft led by Gibson. In the villages and small towns scattered throughout the valley area everything was quiet, the night was calm, the full moon illuminated all the activity clearly enough for many of the inhabitants of the local villages to identify exactly what the bombers were targeting. The targets would soon be decimated and the torrent would be upon them.

The clearest memory, for all those interviewed, is the initial sound of a heavy explosion around 1am on the 17th May. This however, does not specify which crew was dropping their weapon at the time, but it remains probable that this was either Young's or Maltby's 'Upkeep' causing the explosion. Allied to this was the reverberation of the massive Möhne structure capitulating under the stresses caused by the shock waves as the 9,500lb weapons hit their target.

Another possibility is that the loud explosion witnesses heard could have been the loss of Hopgood's aircraft, crashing some three miles from the target.

It seems surprising that the previous explosions, from weapons released by Martin and Gibson had not been heard in the preceding moments.

The sound of the on-rushing torrent of water pushed unrelenting by the sheer volume, it violently cascaded through the valley at fifteen miles per hour and several metres deep.

One witness, Clemens Mols, post-master and resident of Wickede, a village inundated by the torrent, commented that he could see "quite clearly" the waterspout that was created by the explosion of the 'Upkeep' mine against the dam wall. This highlights how clear the moonlit Ruhr Valley was at the time of the attack, as Wickede is approximately fifteen to twenty kilometres downstream from the dam, and seven to eight kilometres east of the Möhne. Mols then explains; the explosion could only have been caused by bombs…Now all remained quiet." The speed of the floods caught everybody in the valley by surprise. The residents closest to the dam especially those resident in the town of Neheim Hüsten and the village of Vosswinkel, which are sited at the confluence of the River Möhne and the River Ruhr. The first time Herr Mols realised that there was impending danger was when he received a telephone call from the post office attendant at Arnsberg, who informed him that "The Möhne barrage is broken, the waters must have reached Vosswinkel, five kilometres away upstream by now."

Mols continues his statement in great detail. It depicts both vividly and graphically the escape bid by himself and his wife. Describing how the water gushed through the windows and doors of his house and rapidly ascended up the stairs, covering the first two metres of the staircase. He suggests that the water level was approximately three metres high outside his house and further down into the valley it was as much as eight meters high. The upper levels of two and three storey dwellings would have been the only floors that would not have been submerged underwater. He also reports the types of debris that the torrent had collected on its journey from the dam, including, a quantity of furniture, wooden beams, a lorry trailer, cattle and human beings, both dead and alive. He even contemplates the possibility that the water may well sweep his house from its foundations. The force of the torrent has picked up or demolished everything in its path. Eye witnesses describe the sound of a steam train as it was enveloped in the torrent and the loud "whizzing" noise that was released by the engine before it was swept away.

The devastation of the onrushing torrent was immense. The timing of the attack, beginning at 1am, local time on the 17th May meant that most residents were asleep or returning to their homes. The lack of aircraft in the area led people to mistakenly assume that it was a false alarm, or another area had been attacked and this was perhaps an all clear signal. Many people, especially those living in the Ruhr had become accustomed to Bomber Command's tactics of high concentration, high altitude bombing. Low flying aircraft,

The canal run up to the dam

Deadly flak firing over the canal leading to the dam

especially heavy bomber aircraft like the Lancaster, were thought to be in difficulty or perhaps on their way to crash after being attacked.

Further upstream, at the Möhne Dam, they had a different perspective as to why the aircraft were at such a low altitude. One eyewitness, known only as Kleeschulte, adamantly notes that he was able to see four aircraft circling over the site. One aircraft, he states, swooped so low it was barely above the surface of the water and this particular aircraft was brightly illuminated. The aircraft, probably Gibson's Lancaster ED932 AJ-G, was commencing its bombing run. The spotlights seemed to have confused Kleeschulte because he continues his statement believing that the aircraft was the same returning after circling the target. This was not the case, as each of the aircraft that he saw was different. In addition, Kleeschulte does not mention the loss of Hopgood and his crew, or the distracting manoeuvres performed heroically by Gibson and Martin to draw enemy fire away from the attacking aircraft. All of these events would have happened within the period that Kleeschulte mentions.

German eyewitness reports, which formed the basis of an official document submitted to the Reich by the Superintendent of Works for the Ruhr Valley Dams Association (Ruhrtalsperrenverein), (the body responsible for the dams and the flow of water to the hydroelectric stations), partly confirm the events of the early hours of the 17th May 1943. The work, by Dr Prüss establishes that the mine Gibson released missed its target due to the weapon becoming embroiled in the protective anti-torpedo netting stretched in front of the wall, about eighty feet away from the face. The bomb exploded near the South Tower. Also confirmed by the eyewitness accounts were the final moments of Hopgood's aircraft. Hopgood attacked the target but released the weapon too late causing it to clear the wall and destroy the power station below. The damaged aircraft attempted to climb but an explosion in the distance confirmed that the pilot had been unsuccessful in his attempts to ditch the aircraft safely. Martin's mine exploded away from the left-hand side of the dam wall causing a massive wall of water to rise into the air. The first thoughts of those positioned at the tower were that the wall had been breached. Young's approach and weapon release caused, according to Prüss' report, "a dull explosion which did not appear to be particularly heavy." Moments later the dam wall would collapse and millions of gallons of water would stream through on its deadly path. There is no mention of Maltby's attack confirming that the dam wall had been breached by Young's weapon alone. Maltby's weapon merely accelerated the process of destruction further.

The anti-aircraft positions in the sluice towers defended the dam vigorously with their inferior weapons before prematurely ceasing fire. Some were killed by the accurate tracer fire of the gunners positioned in the turrets on the aircraft. Others deserted their posts in the knowledge that the target had been breached.

View from the cockpit

Low altitude bombing was a most dangerous task

The Lancasters described by Kleeschulte left a trail of damage in their wake, none of which had ever been witnessed by the residents of the area, even during the worst winter flooding. The breach in the wall between the two sluice towers measured approximately 249 feet in length and 72 feet in depth. The gap was unlikely to have been caused solely by the mines; they simply created fissures in the structure allowing the massive volume of water to escape through them. The damaged rubble and masonry was forced through the gap, continually extending the breach. The torpedo nets, designed to stop any such attack, were simply washed through the gap downstream. The water simply poured through the hole until there was no water situated anywhere but below the level of the breach.     After twelve hours, 116 million cubic metres of the 132 million contained in the vast reservoir had slipped away and was forming the wave which engulfed the towns and villages in its deadly path. Buildings were destroyed over forty miles away. Bridges and other infrastructure were badly damaged over thirty miles away and the water level was reported to be above its normal flow approximately ninety miles downstream of the dam. The 'wave' generated by the flowing tide exceeded fifty feet in height in some of the narrowest valley areas around Neheim. The general flow was thirty feet high and travelling at 15mph. The floods temporarily isolated areas of the city. Roads became rivers and those who dared to make their journeys did so by flat bottomed boats.

Neheim was not alone. The town of Wickede, in which the eyewitness Herr Mols resided, suffered massive amounts of destruction noted in his account. Official reports suggested that the town had been the victim of 'terrible chaos' as the municipal authorities described it. The report suggested twenty-two houses were destroyed. In addition, four factories were destroyed and the road and rail infrastructure of the town completely eradicated. The town lost 117 people and another thirty bodies were washed downstream to towns further along the route.

The devastation of the attack on the Möhne was such that local school children were brought to the worst affected areas to assist in the cleansing operation. Over 2000 additional personnel were drafted into the Neheim and Wickede areas alone.

The aftermath of the attack makes grim reading. Nearly 6,500 cattle and pigs, a vital part of the fertile Ruhr Valley's economy, had been killed and washed miles downstream. Approximately 1000 homes were badly damaged, ninety-two being completely destroyed and almost 1,500[1] people killed in the worst affected areas of the flooding. Official figures showed that the torrent had managed to completely destroy eleven factories, damage 114 more and cause production to cease for a while throughout the whole area. Twenty-five road and railway bridges had been rendered unusable; a further twenty-one were barely passable and would require structural repair. All the local services, gas, water, electricity and pumping stations were rendered inoperable by the attack and the once fertile flood plain of the valley had been ruined. Almost 3,000 hectares of land were now unusable and would remain so for many years.

The same scenario was unfolding in the valley below the Eder Dam. The sound of aircraft in the vicinity was barely noticeable to the inhabitants of the valley. The Allied aircraft often used the lakes, glistening in the moonlight, as a navigational aid. In the village of Hemfurth, inhabitants watched in amazement as the aircraft attacked the dam. Like the residents of the towns and villages surrounding the Möhne, they were unaware of the maelstrom that would career through their town within a matter of minutes.

The actions of the postmaster at Bad Wildungen, situated approximately four miles south of the dam averted catastrophe in some areas. He rang around every village in the area warning of the impending disaster. His actions undoubtedly saved many hundreds of lives that would have been lost.

Unlike the Möhne, the Eder suffered three direct hits against its wall. Shannon's mine cracked the main wall after exploding short of its target. Maudslay's 'Upkeep' again created cracks and loose rubble, but effectively failed to completely breach the target. That honour was left to Les Knight. Knight created a 'V-shaped' breach approximately 229 feet long and 72 feet deep. The thickness of the masonry wall in the area in which the breach occurred was nearly sixty feet.

The Eder, the largest and most important lake in Germany, was at full capacity when the attack took place. The reservoir contained over 202 million cubic metres of water. The breach allowed over 154 million cubic metres, just over three quarters, to escape into the valley below. The flow of water was slower than that recorded at the Möhne, and the larger capacity meant that the lake was still discharging two days after the attack took place. The wave travelled through the valley rarely falling below a height of thirty-eight feet for the first few hours. The floodwaters reached as far as Interschede near the city of Bremen. The town of Interschede is 265 miles downstream from the dam. Even at this distance the effects of the breach saw the town's river levels rise above normal.

Witness reports told of the death and destruction that surged through the villages at perhaps the most vulnerable time for the valley communities, the early hours of the morning. Witnesses' reported seeing bridges, houses, schools and churches being demolished by the onslaught. Many had managed to escape with minutes and seconds to spare.

The first rescue and clear up volunteers described the scene as one of total devastation. Electricity and pumping stations had simply vanished. Houses and villages had disappeared, with little evidence to suggest that any communities had existed on sites directly in the wave's path. A road running parallel with the river basin had subsided continually over a distance of two miles. The towns and cities lying in the Rivers torrent were badly affected also. The wave continued sweeping away everything in the path of its colossal swell, houses, railways stations, track and bridges were all destroyed. The city of Kassel was inundated with two metres of water in the old town district, which lay at low level. The railway and factories, which lay above the floodwaters, weren't hampered in any way. The Allies however, did score successes further downstream. The airfield at Fritzlar was submerged, along with many of the hangar buildings and a railway bridge crossed by the important railway line to Frankfurt was destroyed.

In total, official figures quote the loss of life as forty-seven in the valley area. There were 112 houses washed away and a hundred work places, including those related to heavy industry, destroyed or severely damaged. The river silted pumping stations and once rich agricultural land now stood fallow and unusable and lakes further downstream were severely damaged. Dredging had to be undertaken on inland waterways to allow canal traffic passage to their destination. The disruption to barges stretched over many weeks, severely affecting delivery of essential materials to factories upstream. Whole stretches of major rivers had to have their banks completely rebuilt as most had been eroded by the torrent. There was also a massive loss of cattle and pigs in the area. The damage would cost millions of Marks to repair. Just as had been witnessed at the Möhne, the death and destruction from the attack on the Eder proved more costly to civilians than to heavy industry. The loss of chlorinating plants, water supplies, gas and electricity would affect the region long after the initial blow had been dealt.

Unlike the catastrophe unfolding downstream at the Möhne and Eder. The massive Sorpe Dam was relatively undamaged. The breach that was hoped for did not occur as the sheer size of the dam had prevented any notable damage occurring. Had this dam capitulated like the Möhne and Eder Dams, it would have caused severe disruption to German Industry. The force of the explosion had damaged local houses and destroyed the pumping station in the compensating basin. The attack had caused some minor water seepage, but essentially had failed in its objective.

Albert Speer met officials in Dortmund the following morning after the attack. His major concern was for the restoration of water, gas and electricity supplies to domestic and industrial premises at the first opportunity. Electrical experts were, on his recommendation to Hitler, brought in from around Germany, to assist in the process of restoring essential supplies. In addition, Speer recommended to the Führer that manual labour should be drafted into the area immediately. Arrangements for an initial workforce of 7,000 to divert to the area were made. This would increase within a matter of weeks three-fold. The majority of the workforce would be redirected from the ambitious 'Atlantic Wall project'.

Speer was relieved to learn that the damage was not as catastrophic as he imagined when the Ruhr authorities first informed him. The major difficul-

Wallis' legendary bouncing bomb (between the wheels)

ties would come from relocating workers from other essential projects to over-see the clean up operation. Speer informed the infamous Minister of Information, Göbbels, of his findings. Göbbels attacked the Allied claims of thousands of casualties. He did not blame the Luftwaffe's incompetence for the disaster, unlike Hitler. Instead, Göbbels took the opportunity to assign the blame for the attack squarely at the feet of the Jews. He added, "Now it can be seen how dangerous the Jews are and how right we have been to take them into custody." This standpoint, a clear attempt to diffuse the row concerning the role of the air defences, did not gain much support.

On the 18th May, an article contained in the New York Times revealed that the effect of the raids had not only been the loss of human life, but also to instil fear into the German population at large, convinced that the enemy could cause catastrophic floods at any moment. In addition, it noted that clear signs of civil unrest had been witnessed as fear of an imminent attack gained momentum. Radio stations reported restlessness in major cities across the region as panic gripped the general population. People genuinely feared the next Allied attack. A Reuters' correspondent noted that morale was now at a low ebb and that the damage would not be repaired for at least six months.

The capture of the 'Upkeep' weapon from Barlow's aircraft, ED927 AJ-E, almost undermined the efforts of the British to retain the weapon as top secret. The German scientists quickly began to understand the characteristics of the strange weapon that they had recovered. They did however, overlook the fact that the weapon bounced across the surface, rather than being dropped directly on the target. They identified that the weapon would be rotated at high speed, but wrongly envisaged that this was to develop a level of stability for the aircraft prior to release. Fortunately, political wrangling and the inability to develop an aircraft capable of carrying the weapon hindered the development of a similar German mine to be aimed at British targets.

The aftermath of the attack from a German perspective provides a detailed insight into the moments prior to, during and after the raids had taken place at the Sorpe, Eder and Möhne Dams. It is evident that although the raid did not eradicate the industrial complex as the Air Ministry had hoped it would, it had severely disrupted the manufacture and transportation of essential goods and supplies to the front for some considerable time after the 17th May 1943. As a consequence of the raid, the Reich was damaged and the Allied forces could recoup and plan other devastating offensives against the German heartland once again. The raid was one of many that would target the German war machine until the very last days of the war.

---

[1] This figure contained around 750 POW's, confirmed dead or unaccounted for, who had been housed in a camp downstream from the Dams. The bulk of the casualties were Ukrainian women, with Dutch, French and Polish Nationals also included.

CHAPTER NINE

# *Epilogue*

The 'Dambusters' raid is without doubt one of the most heroic episodes of the entire Second World War. The bravery of the pilots, especially Wing Commander Gibson, the implementation of the project by Wallis and the team at Vickers Armstrong, the persistence of Verity and other members of the Air Ministry, ensured their rightful place in our history books. The episode lives on, both in film and in the media, for present and future generations to digest in admiration of the bravery of the crews undertaking this immensely precarious mission in the heartland of the Third Reich.

The raid was the culmination of years of extensive background research by the Air Ministry into the possibility of hitting German natural resources. Wallis, the genial scientist and inventor was on hand to produce a tangible method of realising the ambitions of the Ministry.

Having had the first design for a high altitude bomb, carried by a specially designed heavy bomber, code named 'Victory', rejected on the grounds of cost (although the idea would be resurrected in part for future operations against German targets under the codenames of 'Tallboy' and 'Grand Slam'), Wallis battled to push his second idea - 'the bouncing bomb'. This project was only made possible with the help of influential people in senior positions. Extensive testing and man hours perfecting the bomb, ensured that it was ready just after the spring rains finished when the dams' water level was at its highest point of the year. The advice and guidance of senior war officials like Charles Portal, undoubtedly brought the war planners to the attention of Wallis' idea. After near rejection for the second time, Wallis was given the opportunity to test his weapon, initially at Chesil Beach, near Weymouth and then in the later stages of development at Reculver Bay, near Margate. The tests initially prove to be disappointing, although structural modifications and alterations to the bomb's delivery eventually paid dividends.

The selection of aircrews, twenty-one in all, seriously deprived other operational squadrons of their most valuable commodities, their pilots and aircrew. The chosen few underwent extensive and hazardous weeks of training in preparation for the attack. Circumnavigating various parts of the country, the crews flew at precariously low altitudes over a period of four weeks, only ceasing their relentless training routine to participate in the raid. However, of the twenty-one initially selected crews, two were unable to fly partly due to a combination of mechanical problems, sickness and an insufficient number of aircraft. This left a total of nineteen specially adapted Lancasters, including the spare used by McCarthy as a result of problems with his Lancaster prior to take-off.

The major question centres on the success of the raid for the Allies. This thought provoking question still remains unanswered, with those who genuinely believe that the raid brought major damage to the Nazis and those who believe that it was perhaps a massive propaganda stunt.

Those who wholeheartedly argue in favour of the raid as a major success in the Allied offensive against the Reich, of whom I consider myself to be, point to the images and aerial reconnaissance photographs supplied after the 17th May 1943. These images give the overwhelming notion that the actions of Gibson and the crews of the nineteen Lancasters had been nothing short of a potentially crippling blow to not only the heartland of German industry, but the spirit and resolution of the German population. The destruction of power stations, farmlands, water supplies and infrastructure would surely have no lesser effect than bringing the suffering of the people to bear upon the belligerent Nazi dictatorship. The war would be over in a matter of months, not years, as the world had witnessed during the attritional Great War of 1914-1918. This, as history shows, was far from the case.

It is transparent that the plan, conceived by the Air Ministry in 1937 and perfected by Wallis in 1943 was a success. The one hundred yard breach across the giant Möhne Dam and the destruction that the ensuing onslaught of 134 million cubic tonnes of floodwater, is concrete proof that his weapon provided the necessary ammunition and desired effect for the Allies. A similar story could be seen a few miles away from the Möhne at the site of the Eder Dam, which had also been breached successfully in the early hours of the 17th May. In this respect, it is seemingly impossible to question the success of the raid and the objectives it achieved.

The argument sits deeply within the notion that the architects of the operation although successful in breaching the dams, did not wholly destroy them as hoped. The bombs worked to the extent that the dams and the valley areas below were dealt a substantial blow. The damage was repaired in a matter of weeks, with the infrastructure either repaired or replaced. The only notable success of the raid was that the repair work meant the proposed construction of the Atlantic Wall, (Hitler's defence against an Allied seaborne invasion into mainland Europe), would be delayed. This was due to the numerous engineers and labourers removed from the coast and reassigned to the dam sites in the German heartland. This was, arguably, a contributing factor to the success of 'Operation Overlord' – the D-Day Landings on June 6th 1944, some 13 months later. However, some historians point to the massive aerial terror bombing campaign against Hamburg and Berlin as more significant in its psychological battle against the German nation, than the raid on the dams. These raids involving both British and US air crews pulverised the major industrial and political centres of the Reich. In Berlin for example, Harris deployed 1000 tonnes of high explosive on the city in twenty minutes in September 1943.

It is easy to see both sides of the argument. The figures and photographs as I have discussed show the destruction caused by 'Upkeep'. The flip side to this argument being that the infrastructure was repaired within weeks and months, albeit only superficially. Aside from the argument, it is clear to see that the operation was a success. The dams were breached, the damage caused by the flooding of the Ruhr Valley was extensive and the psychological effect upon the inhabitants and leadership of Germany was devastating. The mission may not have completely destroyed the targets as was first planned by the Air Ministry and Wallis, but the legacy of the attack would remain stained upon the minds of the German elite. If a raid against such a small, well-hidden target could be accomplished by the RAF, what would stop them from completing similar missions against perhaps even more vulnerable targets. This could be anywhere, not only in German territory, but also in the lands seized by Hitler during the Blitzkrieg operations of 1939 onwards. They could destroy key cities, military establishments, or even targets such as a battleship like the Tirpitz, which was moored, awaiting orders to attack the Atlantic convoys from the Norwegian Fjords. Of course, all of this happened anyway, with key cities such as Hamburg, Berlin and Dresden crushed to the ground, military establishments, including the docks at La Rochelle (the only port large enough to hold the giant battleships of the German Navy). The V2 rocket sites at Peenemunde in August 1943, and the sinking of the Battleship Tirpitz in November 1944 were typical of two major successes, the latter was ironically another of Wallis' masterstrokes. The planned attack on the Battleship Tirpitz, led Wallis to design a weapon that was capable of achieving the aim. This would come in the shape of one of the biggest bombs that Wallis produced for the Allied effort, the 'Tallboy'.

This, I believe, confirms that the raid on the dams was a major success for the Allies, the Air Ministry, the RAF and Wallis. Without the encouragement and faith placed upon him after 'Upkeep', Wallis would have never produced not only the 'Tallboy' weapon, but also the incredible 22,000lb 'Grand Slam'. It is this that provides conclusive proof for the argument that the success of 'Operation Chastise' was perhaps not in its immediate results, but in the long term psychological detriment to the Nazi war machine. The undoubted propaganda coup afforded Bomber Command and the resilience that it gave to the Allied forces and to the war weary population of Britain and the all the Allied nations.

It is difficult to establish whether or not the revolving depth charge shortened the war in any way as was hoped by both Wallis and the Air Ministry. Reservations remain that although unquestionably spectacular and daring in its premise, the attack did not entirely stop the German industrial machine in its tracks, it merely inconvenienced it. The raid did not stop munitions and troops moving to the front lines. In terms of actions that curtailed the war, one must consider D-Day and the poor preparation of troops on the German Eastern Front during the siege of Stalingrad, faced with the onset of the harsh Russian winter looming. The victory in the Battle of the Atlantic and the air supremacy which the Allies enjoyed over Germany towards the end of the conflict, were as important and arguably more significant. It could be argued that the raids against Hamburg, Dresden and Leipzig probably had a greater affect upon the German population's morale Indirectly, 'Operation Chastise' may have been responsible for a shortage of manufacturing and massive collateral damage, but nothing further.

The success of the raid came in the form of a demonstration by the RAF that it could pinpoint and attack vulnerable targets deep within enemy territory. The Third Reich would have to utilise troops and ammunition from other proposed projects to shore up their inadequate defences. The troops and labourers that were brought to the Ruhr from the Atlantic Wall project, for instance and the battalion that may have gone to the front line, now remained in the heartland to protect domestic assets. The undoubted success of the raid is tempered however, by the realisation that from a Squadron of nineteen aircraft and crews, eight Lancasters failed to return, lost in the heat of battle or accidents, bringing a total loss of fifty-three lives. The vision of the Air Ministry and Wallis was to shorten the war and save countless further losses as quickly as possible. However, it would not have escaped them that, although Squadrons were expected to receive combat losses, a rate of over forty percent, if repeated in other raids, would eventually have cost the Allies the war, not won it for them.

The Richard Todd 1954 blockbuster movie rightly celebrated the achievements of Wallis and 617 Squadron for their bravery and determination to make the plan succeed. However, in an era of secrecy, the facts were distorted and the film suffered as a result. The fact that the plans and other details, most notably Wallis' invention the 'Upkeep' mine, were withheld from public gaze is deeply mystifying. The loss of a mine into German hands had eliminated the need for any such secrecy. It had been the Germans who, after reconstructing the damaged bomb, had correctly guessed its purpose and operation, terming it as a 'revolving depth charge'. They could not however, determine how to manipulate the captured weapon for their own use against the Allies. With this weapon in the armoury of the increasingly desperate Third Reich, it would have been a distinct possibility that all the major dams and waterways in Britain would have become legitimate targets for the Luftwaffe. The bomb on the underside of the aircraft was spherical not cylindrical, Gibson was portrayed as a happy go lucky, as 'one of the lads' type of character, when in reality he was a solitary man who commanded respect with a disciplinarian approach. The other crewmembers respected his leadership skills and operational experience, but disliked his dedication which, perhaps unfairly led to the belief that he was arrogant. In the same way, Wallis was unfairly characterised as a slightly insane scientific genius with mistrust and angst against all authority and civil service bureaucracy. The film also depicted the development of the weapon as Wallis' sole responsibility. This is not the case, as without many others connected to research and development and the all-important decision-makers in the Ministry, the plan would not have got off the ground and this truly momentous raid may never have taken place.

The raid provided a massive psychological boost to civilians, not just in Britain, but also those determined to rid their countries of German rule across occupied territory. After years of relentless bombing over London and the destruction of other British cities such as Liverpool and Coventry, this raid came as a timely boost to morale. With the support of the nation, Churchill could carry on the fight against the Nazis intent on invasion and suppression. In the eyes of the Allies, particularly Britain and America, the impregnable German machine had now been penetrated. One point that cannot be overlooked is the actions of the Luftwaffe on the evening of the raid. The Lancasters flew perilously close to major German cities and important strategic targets before reaching their final destination in the Ruhr Valley. The Luftwaffe launched fighters to intercept the Allied aircraft as they progressed deep into German territory. However, they were constrained by their operational abilities at low level and so were unable to engage the Lancasters at such low altitudes. Allied Officials knew this, and planned the attack around the fact that they would encounter little resistance from enemy aircraft en-route.

In a reversal of situations, had Germany attacked the British dams, I believe that the depleted RAF would still have ordered fighters into the night sky to intercept the incoming bombers and destroy them before they reached the target, even at this extremely low altitude. It is interesting to note that no aircraft from 617 was intercepted and destroyed by enemy pilots, all lost aircraft were as a consequence of ground fire or flying accidents. I believe that this highlights the self-denial and arrogance of Hitler and his Commanders in assuming that the Allies were incapable of penetrating their defences and attacking targets with precision flying. Without the tenacity and vision of the Air Ministry and Barnes Wallis, they may well have been correct.

The tide would turn as the Allied offensive gathered pace, bringing the Third Reich to its knees within two years. This legendary raid would provide a catalyst for the Allies to move forward with other offensives that they perhaps would not have contemplated had the Dams Raid never happened in the way they did. There is no doubt that the Dams Raid achieved many results, both physical and psychological, in the UK, amongst the Allies and in Germany. Nevertheless, it should not be forgotten that the dams' raid was but one episode in a long and protracted campaign leading to the final defeat of Germany.

# Appendices

APPENDIX 1

# The Crews

| A/C No | Pilot | Flight Engineer | Navigator | Wireless Operator | Bomb Aimer | Front Gunner | Rear Gunner |
|--------|-------|-----------------|-----------|-------------------|------------|--------------|-------------|
| AJ-ED932-G | WC GP Gibson, DSO | Sgt J Pulford | PO TH Taerum | Flt Lt REG Hutchison | PO FM Spafford | Flt Sgt GA Deering | Flt Lt RAD Trevor-Roper |
| AJ-ED925-M | Flt Lt JV Hopgood | Sgt C Brennan | FO K Earnshaw | Sgt JW Minchin | PO JW Fraser | PO GHFG Goodwin | FO AF Burcher |
| AJ-ED909-P | Flt Lt HBM Martin | PO I Whittaker | Flt Lt JF Leggo | FO L Chambers | Flt Lt RC Hay | PO BT Foxlee | Flt Sgt TD Simpson |
| AJ-ED887-A | Sq Ldr HM Young | Sgt DT Horsfall | Sgt CW Roberts | Sgt LW Nichols | FO VS MacCausland | Sgt GA Yeo | Sgt W Ibbotson |
| AJ-ED864-B | Flt Lt W Astell | Sgt J Kinnear | PO FA Wile | Sgt A Garshowitz | FO D Hopkinson | Sgt FA Garbas | Sgt R Bolitho |
| AJ-ED906-J | Flt Lt DJ Maltby | Sgt W Hatton | Sgt V Nicholsor | Sgt A J Stone | PO J Fort | Flt Sgt V Hill | Sgt HT Simmonds |
| AJ-ED937-Z | Sq Ldr HE Maudsley | Sgt J Marriott | FO RA Urquhart | Sgt AP Cottam | PO MJD Fuller | FO WJ Tytherleigh | Sgt NR Burrows |
| AJ-ED912-N | Flt Lt LG Knight | Sgt REGrayston | FO HS Hobday | Sgt RGT Kellow | FO EC Johnson | Sgt FE Sutherland | Sgt HE O'Brien |
| AJ-ED929-L | Flt Lt DJ Shannon | Sgt RJ Henderson | FO DR Walker | FO CBGoodale | Flt Sgt LJ Sumpter | Sgt B Jagger | PO J Buckley |
| AJ-ED923-T | Flt Lt JC McCarthy | Sgt W Radcliffe | Flt Sgt DA McLean | Sgt L Eaton | Sgt GL Johnson | Sgt R Batson | FO D Rodger |
| AJ-ED934-K | Sgt VW Byers | Sgt AJ Taylor | PO JH Warner | Sgt J Wilkinson | Sgt AN Whitaker | Sgt CMJarvie | Sgt J McDowell |
| AJ-ED927-E | Flt Lt RNG Barlow | Sgt SL Whillis | FO PS Burgess | FO CR Williams | Sgt A Gillespie | FO HS Glinz | Sgt JRG Liddell |
| AJ-ED936-H | PO G Rice | Sgt EC Smith | FO R MacFarlane | Sgt CB Gowrie | Flt Sgt JW Thrasher | Sgt TW Maynard | Sgt S Burns |
| AJ-ED921-W | Flt Lt JL Munroe | Sgt FE Appleby | FO FG Rumbles | Sgt PE Pigeon | Sgt JH Clay | Sgt W Howarth | Flt Sgt HA Weeks |
| AJ-ED886-O | Flt Sgt WC Townsend | Sgt DJD Powell | PO CL Howard | Flt Sgt A Chalmers | Sgt CE Franklin | Sgt DE Webb | Sgt R Wilkinson |
| AJ-ED924-Y | Flt Sgt CT Anderson | Sgt RC Patterson | Sgt JP Nugent | Sgt WD Bickle | Sgt GJ Green | Sgt E Ewan | Sgt AW Buck |
| AJ-ED918-F | Flt Sgt KW Brown | Sgt HB Feneron | Sgt DP Heal | Sgt HJ Hewstone | Sgt S Oancia | Sgt D Allaston | Flt Sgt GS MacDonald |
| AJ-ED910-C | PO W Ottley | Sgt R Marsden | FO JK Barrett | Sgt J Guterman | Flt Sgt TB Johnston | Flt Sgt F Tees | Sgt HJ Strange |
| AJ-ED865-S | FO LJ Burpee | Sgt G Pegler | Sgt T Jaye | PO LG Weller | Sgt JL Arthur | Sgt WCA Long | Flt Sgt JG Brady |

WC – Wing Commander    Sq Ldr – Squadron Leader    Flt Lt – Flight Lieutenant    FO – Flying Officer    PO – Pilot Officer    Flt Sgt – Flight Sergeant    Sgt – Sergeant

APPENDIX 2

# The Crews Who Failed To Return

| Aircraft | Pilot | Take-Off | Crash | Fate |
|---|---|---|---|---|
| AJ-ED937-K | PO VW Byers | 2130 | 2257 | Hit by Flak |
| AJ-ED864-B | FL W Astell | 2159 | 0015 | Hit High Tension cables |
| AJ-ED927-E | FL RNG Barlow | 2128 | 2350 | Hit High Tension cables |
| AJ-ED925-M | FL JV Hopgood | 2139 | 0034 | Crippled by 'Upkeep' blast*? |
| AJ-ED865-S | PO LJ Burpee | 0011 | 0200 | Hit by Flak |
| AJ-ED910-C | PO W Ottley | 0009 | 0235 | Hit by Flak? |
| AJ-ED937-Z | SL HE Maudsley | 2159 | 0236 | Crippled by 'Upkeep' blast** |
| AJ-ED887-A | SL HM Young | 2147 | 0258 | Hit by Flak |

* Lancaster hit by flak on approach causing 'Upkeep' to be dropped late, the explosion severely injured Hopgood and led to the aircraft crashing nearby

** Lancaster had a difficult approach to the target and bomb release delayed causing aircraft to be caught in the resulting explosion  Maudsley bravely tried to return to Scampton in the badly damaged aircraft but was hit by flak approaching the Dutch border

? Two crewmembers managed to evacuate the aircraft before it crashed  These were Sergeant Minchin and Pilot Officer Burcher who were subsequently captured and imprisoned by the German authorities

? One member of the crew survived the crash  Rear Gunner, Sergeant Tees was badly injured and captured  Having survived the war, he died in 1982 and his ashes taken to the Reichswald Forest War Cemetery to lie with his crewmates

APPENDIX 3

# *Chronology of Events*

**1937**

1 October     Western Air Plans drafted by the Air Ministry, including WA5, which was directly concerned with attacking Industrial production of the Ruhr Valley

**1938**

20 July     Wallis meets with Beaverbrook, the Minister for Aircraft Production and discusses his plans for attacking the Ruhr Industrial complex utilising a large earth-penetrating bomb and a specially designed high altitude bomber aircraft

August     Wallis is given permission to utilise the facilities at the National Physics Laboratory for testing the design of his weapon in a wind tunnel

October     Road Research Laboratory in Middlesex uses 1:50 scale model of the Dams to test the feasibility of Wallis' hypothesis

**1941**

March     A note on a method of attacking the Axis powers' treatise released by Wallis outlining his plan for the bomb and Victory aircraft

May     Air Ministry Officials reject outright the Wallis theory considering it to be a huge waste of time and effort for a single operation

**1942**

April     A determined Wallis begins to make rudimentary tests on a new bouncing bomb, which he believes, would be the most practical way of targeting the Ruhr Valley Dams  Wallis is given approval to begin testing his new theory at the National Physics Laboratory after encouragement from both the Air Ministry and the Admiralty

May     The first of the explosive charge tests is carried out at the disused Nat-Y-Gro Dam in mid-Wales

4 December     First dropping test of the spherical weapon undertaken at Chesil Beach near Weymouth on the Dorset coast

15 December     Second trial undertaken at Chesil Beach

**1943**

9 January     Third trial at Chesil Beach  Wallis' second treatise, 'Air attack on Dams is published

23 January     Fourth Trial undertaken

5 February     Fifth test completed

23 February     Wallis told in no uncertain terms (by the Chairman of Vickers Armstrong, Craven) to cease with the idea of attacking the Dams. Linnell, the Controller of Research and Development at the Ministry of Aircraft Production had given the order.  Wallis immediately offered to resign his position at Vickers Armstrong

| 26 February | Linnell reverses the decision he had made a few days previously  Wallis was too be given anything that was required to make the tests a success |
| 15 March | On completion of a long tour of duty with 106 Squadron, Wing Commander Guy Gibson is posted to 5 Group Headquarters at Grantham |
| 17 March | Squadron X is formed and posted to RAF Scampton in Lincolnshire |
| 24 March | Squadron X officially renamed as 617 Squadron  With many of the crews already stationed at the site, 10 borrowed Lancaster's are made available to train the crews for low flying exercises |
| 13 April | First scale 'Upkeep' tests undertaken at Reculver Bay near Margate in Kent using cylindrical weapon covered in wooden outer casing |
| 18 April | Second test conducted after removal of troublesome outer-casings |
| 21 April | Third test undertaken |
| 1 May | The fourth test undertaken using full scale cylinder |
| 10 May | 'Highball' trials in Scottish Lochs are abandoned after disappointing results obtained during testing |
| 16 May | Nineteen Lancaster's prepare for take-off from Scampton; destination the Ruhr.  Over the next few hours three waves of aircraft would depart at intervals to attack the Dams of the Ruhr Valley |
| 17 May | Lancaster's return to Scampton after successfully breaching two of the three primary targets and attacking other secondary targets  Eight aircraft failed to return |

APPENDIX 4
# Bibliography

### Books

Brickhill, Paul '*The Dam Busters*', Rev Ed Bell & Hyman Limited, London 1978

Chorley, WR '*Bomber Command Losses of the Second World War 1943, Vol 4*', Midland Counties Publishing 1996, pp 151-152

Cooper, Alan '*Born Leader – The Story of Guy Gibson VC*', Independent Books, London 1993

Cooper, Alan '*The Men Who Breached The Dams – 617 Squadron The Dam Busters*' 2nd Ed Airlife, Shrewsbury 1993

Cooper, Alan W '*The Air Battle of the Ruhr – RAF Offensive March to July 1943*' Airlife, Shrewsbury 1992

Delve, K & Jacobs, P '*The Six-Year Offensive – Bomber Command in World War II*', Arms & Armour, London pp 126-135

Hecks, Karl '*Bombing 1939-45 – The Air Offensive against Land Targets in World War II*' Robert Hale Publishing, London 1990; pp 169-170

Middlebrook, Martin '*The Peenemünde Raid*' Allen Lane Publishing, London

Middlebrook, Martin & Everitt, Chris '*The Bomber Command War Diaries – An Operational Reference Book – 1939-45*' Viking Publishing, London 1985 pp 386-388

Sweetman, John '*The Dambusters Raid*', 2nd Ed Arms & Armour, London 1990


### Public Records Office
Air 14 – 840
Air 14 – 2088
Air 14 – 2144
Air 14 – 844
Air 8 – 1234


### Royal Airforce Museum, Hendon

B 483            – A note on a method of attacking the Axis Powers

AC72/23          – Papers of Wing Commander F W Winterbotham

(Unaccessioned)  – Papers of Group Captain Conrad Verity

X002-4908        – Target folder for Eder Dam

006409           – Log book of Wing Commander G P Gibson

B1086            – Nine eye witness reports of the attack on the Möhne Dam by 617 Squadron 15/5/1943

AC71/2/25-28     – Reconnaissance photographs of the three Dams

PC71/19/341/1-2  – Reconnaissance photographs

PC71/19/795-799  – Reconnaissance photographs

PC71/19/356/1-114 – Ground-level photographs

X002-5655        – Wehrmacht report on air attacks on the Möhne, Eder and Sorpe Dams, 1943